Beaten Black and Blue

Born into Racism

AUGUSTE KNUCKLES

authorHOUSE®

AuthorHouse™ UK
1663 Liberty Drive
Bloomington, IN 47403 USA
www.authorhouse.co.uk
Phone: UK TFN: 0800 0148641 (Toll Free inside the UK)
       UK Local: 02036 956322 (+44 20 3695 6322 from outside the UK)

Published by AuthorHouse 09/17/2020

ISBN: 978-1-6655-8022-9 (sc)
ISBN: 978-1-6655-8023-6 (hc)
ISBN: 978-1-6655-8021-2 (e)

Print information available on the last page.

This book is printed on acid-free paper.

Dedicated to my wife and our amazing children
I've been truly blessed.

CONTENTS

ABOUT THE AUTHOR

To have achieved the unachievable, to have finally spoken out and written these words, I sincerely hope my story gives victims, survivors of abuse and neglect courage. Regardless, don't let anyone tell you, you can't achieve great things no matter how big the obstacle. Auguste Knuckles 1st time author, who really doesn't consider himself an Author by the way.

THE END OF THE BEGINNING

January 2020, the day my world came crashing down around me. The cold dark blanket of suicide once again having its day, but this day he was all guns blazing. Thoughts so loud, thoughts so disturbing, telling me it would be over quickly; it would be quick, easy, and painless. *Nothing to worry about,* my thoughts were telling me. *Nothing to worry about.*

I'd never experienced anything as powerful or overwhelming as what was going on in my head, a full-blown, lightspeed, psychotic meltdown. *Just pull the car over onto the hard shoulder, exit the car, and walk head-on into rush hour traffic on the M25. Quick, easy, and painless. I promise you, this is as good as it gets. This is your time.*

Leaving behind a world I had struggled so hard to build, a world that was my wife and our beautiful children. My world that had given me so much love, something I seldom experienced as a child.

I thought my war had ended when I returned from the Middle East in 1991 having served as a soldier, a desert rat, during the first Gulf War. I was awarded a commendation by the commanding chief of the Allied Forces, the Gulf War medal and clasp, plus the liberation of Kuwait medal, all of which I sold to feed my addiction.

A dyslexic punching bag, a loner who had no place at school or at home, I found purpose through food. Classically trained, I went on to forge a career in the hospitality industry, working my way up the ladder to be executive head chef in some of the busiest and most prestigious hotels and restaurants in the United Kingdom.

After I had finally won the battle with drugs and alcohol, another war had started, my war with mental health. It would have been easier to have put that bullet through my brain during the war. It's a war I'm still fighting to this day, diagnosed with complex post-traumatic stress disorder (CPTSD), anxiety, and obsessive-compulsive disorder (OCD) and all its side orders. I'm a fragile soul believe it or not, but I'm a survivor.

Writing this book hasn't been easy, but it has helped me put closure to some of my darkest flashbacks and nightmares. You see, I'm just the average guy on the street, trying to make his way through this complex enigmatic labyrinth called life. There was no way I was going to let my challenges stop me from telling my story. *Beaten Black and Blue* is the true story of my life.

AMUSE BOUCHE

When I sit and ponder my life as a boy, it brings tears to my eyes. What would I say if I could go back and speak with that scared, frightened little fella, if I could go back in time? "Run, hide, call the police, tell a family member, call a friend, tell a teacher." I was a child, I didn't know what to do. I find it hard to believe that no one saw the bruises, heard the cry for help, or saw the sadness behind my cheeky smile as a four-year-old boy. If the truth be told I believe they all saw what they decided to ignore, me.

I would say, "You will most certainly overcome the pain, but the biggest challenge will be dealing with the trauma as you grow through the decades into manhood and finally have children of your own."

It's been a turbulent journey, countless highs and lows, battling addiction, depression, anxiety, and my demons within. It has, in fact, been brutal suffering in silence, but I'm no longer frightened or unsure of what the future holds.

At the age of forty-something, I've finally found my voice. I've finally found a way to cope with the flashbacks, nightmares, and the mental, emotional, and physical abuse inflicted on me by the ones who should have protected me from harm. One could say I've found inner peace with the cold dark blanket of suicide, the last exit for so many lost souls.

I've finally willed the courage to speak. I've finally confessed to loved ones why I was disconnected, distant, fractured, and lost. It wasn't meant to be this way, I myself have hurt those closest to me, but others had a heavy hand that rained down on me. I'm not perfect,

3

but if you smash a Ming vase and super glue it back together, its not going to be the same vase.

If I could go back and speak with those abusers and the ones who stood silently in the shadows and did nothing, what would I say? I wouldn't say anything. My life has been a rollercoaster of miracles, all of you who have lived in my shadow these past decades and witnessed the beauty which I have miraculously created and what I have experienced. It's all my abusers who have become silent, knowing that my presence in their lives is me tolerating every breath they take.

My journey of healing still requires ongoing therapy, medication, and assessments with various psychologists and doctors. My future has a new horizon, positive vibes, family and friends around me who love me and want to see me happy and healthy. If asked what has been achieved this past four decades, the cycle of hereditary abuse has finally been broken, and it was the unfortunate luck of a fragile four-year-old boy who did it.

This cooking malarkey has almost killed me, AK

SPROUTS

S prouts, what's the big deal with sprouts. As a chef during the festive season, having taste for a good sprout goes along way, especially when cooking for thousands of Christmas party guests. I would get my commis chefs to check that they were cooked and seasoned well before plating. A well-cooked sprout can either break or make a Christmas dinner. During my childhood, they would break me every single time Doris served them.

When I initially began to write this book, I remember every second, third, fifth word would either be "fuck", "cunt", "bastard", "wanker", or "twat". Swear words just poured out of me with such venom, coursing through my veins until finally released via my fingertips. I just held my head in my hands thinking, *why am I even thinking, let alone trying to complete such a project?* The fact I'm dyslexic made me very anxious. Thank god for spell check.

I suppose I wasn't mentally, emotionally, or physically ready to embark on such a journey. If the truth be told, I don't think I had truly processed the anger or the agony within. I don't think I will ever come to terms with my childhood, although I will have to process what has held me back all these years, addiction. All I pray and work for today is that I find some sort of peace within myself and be a true inspiration to my children.

My question to this day is, if you have a child who doesn't like a certain food item, why go to all the trouble persecuting them for hours on end at the dinner table in trying to force them to consume such an item?

I just didn't like sprouts, regardless of who cooked them or how they were cooked. I just had no love whatsoever for the humble baby cabbage. Over the decades of explaining the traumatic episode during my childhood to family and friends, the only comparison is the Russian roulette scene in one the most epic movies ever made, *The Deer Hunter.*

Sunday morning would start with our visit to church, Sunday school. I suppose it was the only chance for my parents to get a leg over living in such a small council house on the estate where we lived during the eighties. Five kids and two adults crammed into a three-bed semi-detached house like hundreds of other families living on the breadline.

One thing I did like about Sunday school was volunteering to go around and take up the collection. Main reason was I would skim at least a fiver from the collection to spend on sweets, custard creams, and crap during the school week. I'll go into that a bit later. Savage I know robbing from the church, I suppose that's why I like to give folding money as opposed to coins during Sunday mass today, my way of asking for forgiveness. Apologies you never got that new church roof.

Arrive home from church then off to the corner shop to buy cider and barley wine for Doris, and whatever else she needed to get through her day. I would make two or three journeys before and after dinner. Cider, I say. Yes, a ten-year-old off to buy alcohol for the grown-ups.

If the neighbours knew I was off to the shop, they would shout over the garden fence, "Oi treacle, can Deliveroo pick me up ten B&H and four cans of special brew?" Procuring fags and alcohol at the ripe old age of ten had been going on for a few years, so do the math, drink responsibly. Fuck that shit back in the eighties, all you shabby parents should have procured responsibly before considering a 24hr lock in.

So, she's in the kitchen, preparing and cooking dinner, smashed off her chops with a jaw at 9 o'clock. May I say for the record the kitchen on Sundays was out of bounds. If you did manage to get in, you would be met with a scolding slap with the wooden spoon that had sat in a pot of gravy for the best part of an hour.

Not only would you have a wooden spoon print across your chops for the remainder of the day, you would be scalped with the most horrific verbal abuse: "Get the fuck out the kitchen, you scroungy little bastard. Go on, fuck off. That's it, get the fuck out of the kitchen." Strange considering I didn't even get a foot in.

So, things are cooking up nicely before we go full wankered, full-on abuse is in the post for the kid who has no love whatsoever for baby cabbages. "Are we having sprouts?" I've spent many years trying to put into perspective what was going on in the household kitchen every Sunday. Lines of coke, a massive joint hanging out the kitchen window. Were there other people in there having a party? maybe I'll never know.

Five minutes before service there is a mad panic around the place, like a dysfunctional kitchen before service—mayhem, carnage, kids pull the table out, get it laid. Mad panic, me and my three siblings running around the gaff like headless waiters with two left feet. But who's got the balls to enter the kitchen to fetch the cutlery? The black sheep of the family has, though he's more like forced to enter the dreaded fortress. Shoved through the door by the ravaged hungry mod, gagging for lumpy mash.

I always used to think Doris was a decent chef, but looking back, I would be traumatised every other meal I was served. I remember sitting on a plastic chair, food thrown in front of us like we had to be grateful for what we were about to consume. Grateful. Grateful was beaten out of me every given chance. More like resentment for what I was forced to eat.

I don't ever remember meat being on my plate, was us kids' vegans? I always remember a juicy piece of meat being on Boris's plate. We've all witnessed a hungry dog attacking a bowl of dog meat; the dog goes bananas. Well imagine four starving kids going off over a plate of veg, mash, and lumpy gravy. My siblings would put a plate of food away in seconds while Boris lavished over his prime cut of whatever Doris happened to have purchased from the butchers.

Then the sprouts, food of the devil. This was when two bottles of cider and half a dozen cans of barley wine would kick in. I'd push the sprouts around my plate for the best part of thirty minutes. "Eat those fucking sprouts or else".

"I've worked my ass off for you stinking kids to put food on the fucking table," said Doris. As if I knew what a hard day's work was like. It was totally irrelevant how hard she had worked for a child to comprehend. Why would she be so fixated in trying to force-feed me something I couldn't stomach?

Three siblings polished off their food, slurp, slurp. Bosh, job done. "Please, I don't like the taste of sprouts mom".

"You're an ungrateful little bastard. You will not leave this table until those sprouts are eaten." Another thirty minutes pass. Cold sprouts. Boris splayed out on the couch, pushing out z's as loud as a jet. Siblings out in the yard playing ball. Another thirty minutes pass. She's on me like a rat on a Big Mac. In my face, her eyes blazing with hatred. "You fucking eat them now."

Sitting at the table with a revolver at my temple, scared as a kid riding the Pepsi max. A sick, twisted Doris in my face, sweating like a dyslexic on countdown, eyeballs glazed over. "Eat those fucking sprouts!" Palm of her hand smashes on the table. She must be warming up. I'd long gone pissed myself. Sodden, I'm frozen, crouching over a plate of cold sprouts, unable to speak let alone breathe.

I start to hyperventilate; an asthma attack is clearly on its way. Stressed beyond measure, whimpering, "I don't like sprouts," has no effect, I'm now full blown in her vortex.

The mad, crazed Vietnamese soldier is going off "Doris". A week in the bamboo cage submerged in a rat-infested waterway is looking inviting. I need to get off this table, out of this nightmare. Before I know it, she screams, "Right, fuck off to bed." One nil to Doris. Playtime is long gone, siblings back indoors. It's in the bath, one boiled kettle between four of us.

I remove myself from the empty table the size of a football pitch. Doris is slurping the last dregs from her cider bottle, mangled on the sofa. I haven't the energy to strip naked and climb into a bath of cold mud. I climb to the top bunk exhausted, shamed, lost. I cry myself to sleep knowing next Sunday will be the same barbaric insanity.

"Daddy."

"Yes, son?"

"I don't like sprouts."

"It's okay. I haven't put any on your plate."

"Thank you, Daddy. I love you."

YOU'RE IN THE ARMY NOW BOY

Fuck me what do we have here? A gollywog, the only gollywog in this squadron. From now on during training you are going to be known as jigaboo, do you here me boy? Yes sergeant, he's no place on this parade square, he marches like a monkey.

BOOT-POLISH BLACK

During long hot summers back in the eighties, I couldn't sleep at night due to my asthma, It was difficult at times. Doris always insisted I go to bed with my younger siblings. My elder sister would be out and about, hanging out with other teenagers her age, black, white, mixed-race, Asian, and ethnic kids. Black like me, brown just like me.

As soon as my siblings fell asleep, I would sneak out of bed, crawl along the landing, hide or be as invisible as possible, and watch TV from the top of the stairs. Haven't a clue what I'd be watching, thinking about it, most likely racist comedians, telling jokes about anyone who wasn't like them, but I would sit there. Any decent mother would have known I was at the top of the stairs and most likely would have invited me down—if I was on my best behaviour and I didn't make a sound.

I heard Boris and Doris talking in the living room, the thought today makes me sick. The pair of them plotting their assault on my sister when she returned home. The estate was multicultural, and my sister hung out with likeminded teenagers like herself, we didn't no racism, we were born into it. You only know it's meaning when you are old enough to understand the magnitude of the word.

Just for the record, Boris and Doris were white. My two younger siblings, half siblings, were white. My older sister was white, I was black, "half-breed", "mixed-race", "crusty". Although I hadn't a clue what my heritage was, so I can't go there at this stage.

There was a knock at the door. I was still watching whatever I was watching from the top of the stairs. I hear him ask Doris, "Are you ready?" Most likely he's given her a wink and a nod for confirmation that she's okay with the barbarian punishment about to be laid down.

My sister hadn't even stepped foot in the house when she was grabbed by the scruff of her neck and dragged through the door two feet off the ground. For the record, I need to mention this bully of a man, Boris, isn't even her father. The woman sat on her drunken, twisted, sick, and toxic ass is her biological mother.

I didn't get it then, and I will never understand how or why Doris would allow her child to be beaten up by a man who was not even the father. What kind of woman would you have to be to allow this to happen. It was carnage—pure, unadulterated carnage—and I sat at the top of the stairs, witnessing this in my own home.

Decades later, Doris would cower behind a large glass of whisky or wine and blame him. Yes, she blamed Boris. No, she let this happen, and to this day, I'm convinced she probably got some sort of twisted pleasure witnessing two of her children being battered. If not, why didn't she put herself between him and me and my elder sister. Why didn't she say, "No! Don't you fucking dare touch my kids"?

My sister was dragged into the kitchen, screaming, "Let me go." I was frozen, still invisible at the top of the stairs. I can hear my sister's screams to this day, Doris did nothing. She just sat on her ass, on her sofa.

He grabbed the black shoe polish from beneath the sink. My sister screamed, "No! Leave me alone. Don't do it. Please, please, Mom help me!" Once he got hold of the polish, my sister would be dragged into the living room, still screaming. Then he would rub black boot polish into her face.

I couldn't do anything, I was scared, totally and utterly frozen. Should I have gone downstairs and pleaded with him to stop, no, because guaranteed he would lay into me. After all, he had laid into me for less when I was a child.

"You want to hang out with those black fucking losers, darkies" he would shout, "maybe we should paint you fucking black, so you can be like them." A wooden spoon would be broken over her back.

Boot polish all over my sister's face, tears—so many tears—and cries for help, but she just sat there.

I'd run back to my bunk and try and hide under the bedsheets scared, so scared, that he would continue his rage and come upstairs. I lost count how many times this happened over the years. It was surreal, but this was going on; it was going on. I started to have issues with the colour of my skin. I was having issues with my identity, issues with me being me. I began to hate myself for being black because I saw what my sister was subjected to because of boys like me. It was the ultimate head fuck for a child to witness. I felt worthless, I wanted to die.

Having children of my own with the most amazing wife, I just can't and will never understand why a parent would want to beat down on their children. I know it happens, and it's fucking wrong on all levels. Knowing full well they will be left with emotional, mental, and physical scars for the remainder of their lives. Or was it just an eighties thing. No, it wasn't just an eighties thing. This was the result of generational abuse, on a level engraved so deep. Her life had taken on a direction that I believe she still regrets to this day, when she lay with my biological father. Regret, she sought closure by allowing the abuse of her children by a sick and twisted individual, as if I was the one to blame for her shenanigans.

Now I'm not going to say I was an angel by any means. I was dealing with serious issues, so when I was given advice to seek help, I went and got help, took me a few years, but I got help. You can lead a donkey to water, but whether he decides to drink that water is down to the donkey. I drank the water. Not the donkey's water, but you know where I'm coming from.

Doris had the audacity to sit there crying, usually at family get-togethers with the biggest audiences. Obviously drunk, she would make out she was the victim. "I couldn't do anything", she would mumble from behind her glass, expecting all of us to feel sorry for her. She *didn't* do anything. Doris could have prevented the beatings and abuse. She knows full well that lying blatantly through her teeth doesn't cut it anymore, not with me anyways.

It's a bit late in life, after you've been to hell and back and then gone back for more, to want to be subjected to more lies on the other end of a phone call, listening to someone wanting to tell you she's sorry. Sorry, really? This boy is already baked. You can't go back adjust a few ingredients and pop him back in the oven, no, not unless your Marty Mcfucking Fly

I see hundreds of thousands of people protesting that black lives matter in the world today. Racism shouldn't exist, but it does. As a dual-heritage man, I can't help but go back to the top of those stairs in that toxic putrid house, on that god-forsaken estate we were dragged up and not think about my life. I was born into racism and have witnessed it first-hand within the family who raised me, so how could I not be affected, affected is an understatement, so yes, if asked, do black lives matter, hell yeah. #BLM

TWENTY-FIRST BIRTHDAY COCKTAIL, AMSTERDAM.

Ingredients

1 gram of PCP
2 grams cocaine
6 Love doves
4 LSD tads banana splits
2 grams speed
1 bottle Jack Daniels
8 tumblers
1 ounce of purple haze for the journey
1 Defibrillator

Method

Take all ingredients except Jack Daniels, purple haze and defibrillator, crush in a pestle and mortar. When all ingredients are combined, divide between tumblers. Fill the glasses with Jack Daniels and consume. I would strongly suggest you do not try this dish unless you are accompanied by an adult.

GOLD FISH

At the depths of addiction, there is no line to cross, there are no boundaries, there is no filter, no man's land is all around you. The world inside your goldfish bowl, with a broken windscreen wiper screeching as it rubs across the glass bowl on the outside is the only thing that makes sense, that and doing more cocaine. The world around you is plugged into a moon sized speaker, jacked up, the quiver travels through you at lightning speed, unable to string a sentence together, you stand silent, drinking yourself into a coma. **AK**

ABANDONED

'm a chef by trade, I've been cooking professionally since the age of seventeen. That's when I started my first proper paid job within Her Majesty's Forces, Army Catering Corp (ACC). The ACC no longer exists; the army bought in contractors. It's a shame. Although we were called 'slop jockeys', we cooked some seriously good-quality food for the boys.

Considering there was never much about the household when we were kids, and that number two always had different food than us kids at mealtimes, food seemed so appealing to me, "why wouldn't it black Olive Twist". The love for food came about during my home economics classes at school. I would rock up to class with a bag of whatever I could scrounge from around the house or shoplift from the local corner shop. At the end of class, I would have made either spring rolls, some sort of Chinese stir fry, a gateau or sponge cake decorated with buttercream, fresh fruit, and chocolate garnishes.

Long story short, my home economics teacher spoke with Doris during the school holidays. Then boom, I was enrolled at the catering community college across town. I enrolled in 1985 and studied classical French cuisine, patisserie, and food and beverage service for the hospitality industry.

General Certificate of Secondary Education (GCSE)
English—ungraded
History—ungraded
Maths—ungraded

Rural Science—ungraded

Craft Design Technology—ungraded

Home Economics Theory—ungraded, practical (pass)

If you subject a child to extreme levels of mental, physical, and emotional abuse, there will be some serious issues with school. This showed in my school grades and when I did finally leave school. In the words of so many teachers and my dysfunctional family, I was going to be a loser, a nobody, a dead beat.

It makes me laugh today. My uncle Henry, as flash as he was back then with the sports cars, the cool designer clothes his lavish lifestyle, was the only one laughing and joking about me being beaten black and blue, when he visited us. Where is Henry today? On the fucking bread line, picking litter off the street.

I had zero confidence throughout my teens, no self-esteem, no willpower to do anything. If it wasn't for my home economics teacher, Mrs Buxton, bless her soul, I would have most likely drifted in and out of trouble and juvenile centres. I most likely would have ended up in a young offender's centre, last stop prison, most likely spending many years as someone's wife and then on to an early grave.

Thinking about it, back then Doris never encouraged me to do anything, nothing, and I mean fuck all. She might have dragged me uptown a few times to carry shopping bags and forced me to join the army cadets, but apart from that, there wasn't much going on.

As a chef I've worked in some amazing restaurants with Michelin-star chefs, stunning hotels across the globe, and cruise ships. I have been fortunate to have travelled extensively. I also ran my own restaurant in Spain for two years with two business partners I met working as a private chef in the Alps circa 2000.

In 2016 I was working at a beautiful hotel in Marlow as a pastry chef, something different than my usual line of employment as an executive head chef. I think I just needed a change to get me out the office and away from doing all the mundane jobs we executive head chefs hate but had to do. Budgets, forecasting, meetings, strategizing, Human resources, development and meetings about meetings, plus getting extremely smashed at staff parties. I needed to get back to some form of cooking, get back to my love for food.

Working through an agency, the pay wasn't bad, but nothing like I'd earned before. How I saw it was if the bills were covered, there was food on the table, and I had change for petrol, I was happy taking orders from someone else for a change. Not having much responsibility, able to create beautiful desserts, afternoon teas, and assist with weddings and functions across the estate was a winner.

I had been at the hotel for several months, and our second child, was cooking nicely in the wife's belly oven. I can't remember the exact date, but I received a phone call from a prestigious agency for chefs regarding a vacant position in a beautiful, four-star, deluxe hotel in the West Midlands.

My résumé was online on various social media platforms. You must keep yourself out there as you never know which general manager is looking for a well-seasoned, experienced, down-to-earth, open-minded, hands-on chef to revitalize their culinary department.

Several phone calls and three interviews later, plus several discussions with my wife about working away from home for a few years, I was finally appointed the new executive head chef for the beautiful property. I started employment in the third quarter of 2016.

I travelled up the M40 from Berkshire to Birmingham first thing Monday morning and did what chefs do—meetings, strategizing, menu development, forecasting and budgeting, scheduling, speaking with clients and suppliers, and the odd bit of cooking. I then travelled back down the M40 Friday afternoons. Sometimes I cruised down the M1 to mix up the scenery a little. The M40 can be a drag; it's as flat as Belgium.

The one condition I was hesitant about in taking this new position on was having to move back in with Doris as the hotel was a short drive from her house, it was the only sensible option, otherwise I would have to rent an apartment near the hotel. So, to save a few grand I moved in during the week.

Moving back into my old bedroom was going to have its challenges. The main one was getting on with Doris again. Or maybe it would be a chance for her to explain herself as to why I was battered left, right, and centre, how wrong was I? I had more chance of making love to a merman.

The first few months flew by. Doris was now married to Alfred and a carer for her mother, the one and only evil Phillis, a former member of the SS death squad. By the way if there are any Nazi hunters out there this isn't true. Its just the anger within me trying to express what she did and how I feel about her. Phillis was in full-blown dementia. She wore a nappy at night and during the day, dressed in her designer clothes, sat propped up in her chair in the naughty corner. There she sat day in day out, month after month, year after year. Phillis often called me her son. Or she would ask, "Look at the handsome young man. Who is he? What's he doing here? Is it Christmas?" Dribble, dribble, more dribble. She thought I was her father at one stage and a past lover. Although dementia was having its day, Phillis knew everything going on under her nose.

Doris and Alfred loved a drink, and I mean "a drink." They were often on the pop from the crack of dawn until they crashed in the afternoon. Often when I arrived home after an early shift, it wasn't surprising if they were all tucked up by 5 p.m. with a leftover takeaway of some sort in the dog bowl.

What I witnessed during my time back at that house absolutely set in concrete how angry and sometimes evil Doris was. I often arrived home after work tired and needed to rest. But she would be going off, going off the fucking rails, lost the fucking plot, mental going off. Doris screamed abuse at Alfred. "Get away from me you fucking cunt".

On and on and on, who the fuck are you? You fucking disgust me, you fucking horrible bastard." She would also lose it with Phillis, and I mean physically and mentally abuse the old lady. Regardless, it's not on. Doris would of course, also lose it with me, screaming up the stairs to my room, "You're no fucking good either, you fucking bastard, who the fuck do you think you are, you can fuck off out of here, ya bastard". Sheer hatred and anger pouring out from her mouth, it was savage at times, some nights I Just left and slept in the hotel, leaving her to continue her onslaught.

It's ironic after what Phillis did all those decades back that she forced her grown daughter to give me up, yet I was there, standing between them both, shouting at Mother to calm the fuck down and back off, or I'd call the police and social services if the abuse didn't stop. Phillis in a care home, a *One Flew over the Cuckoo's Nest*–type place, and Doris banged up in solitary for being a nutter, a lunatic.

Now what I'm about to say hasn't been dressed up like a beautiful line-caught salmon, poached, garnished, and ready for a million-dollar banquet. It's the truth. Just for the record, I had no intention back then, when shacked up with Murdock in writing a book. My only intention was to do well within my employment and embrace my wife and kids when I arrived home Friday afternoons.

Every other week and obviously smashed on grapes, during conversation Doris would mumble, "They made me do it. They fucking made me do it, fucking bastards."

"Made you do what? What the fuck did they make you do? Who made you do what?" I would ask.

"Tell him, tell him the truth," Alfred would say. But she never did. This bullshit went on for months, until one evening I sat with her and asked her face-to-face, "What the fuck did they make you do?"

"What the fuck are you going on about. Made you do what?" Then out it came.

"When you were born, I had to take you to my parents' house because I had nowhere to go after I knifed him in the face with a kitchen knife."

"What the fuck? Knifed your then husband in the face? Fuck me. Talk about a psycho."

"We just had to go there, you, me, and your sister. But my parents, your grandparents, persecuted me every day about having a black baby in the house. They couldn't stand having you there. You were a shame on the family,"

This was just bonkers but considering the climate in the United Kingdom in the early seventies, mixed-marriages and half-breed kids in some circles were not good for morale. Not good at all. I had been born into a family of Enoch Powell supporters, BNP, you name it. It wouldn't surprise me if Phillis had a picture of the man himself hanging in the kitchen, Enoch or Adolf.

How can a baby be a shame on the family? I mean seriously. This went on for months and months. "They fucking hated you being in there house, so they gave me an ultimatum," Doris told me. "Can you fucking believe this? Well this isn't Hollywood, people. This isn't *Different Strokes*. We both leave, or you leave."

"Leave me? Leave me where? Where would I leave to? Where would a baby go? Nightclubbing? It's not like I could make a few sandwiches, wrap them in a handkerchief, and head on out the door like Huckleberry Finn on one of his merry adventures through KKK country."

My blood started to boil. My pulse became erratic, and beads of sweat poured from my brow because the bitch who orchestrated this—Phillis—sat in the next room. The woman I had defended from her own daughter not even a month ago, the fucking SS commander and racist bitch, sat dribbling in the next room, thinking I was her ex-lover.

"So, what did you do."

"I abandoned you."

"What do you mean, you abandoned me? What, like wrapped me in a blanket and left me outside a charity shop with a sign around my neck, 'Please help me'?"

"Your grandparents."

"Stop. No, no, stop there. They couldn't be my grandparents. They're savages."

"They just couldn't bear the thought of sharing their household with a baby like you". We drove to Johnny's barracks. He was waiting at the gates, and I just handed you to him and walked away." I'm fucking gobsmacked. "I handed you, my baby, to him like a packed fucking lunch. You were screaming, screaming so loud Auguste everyone was watching. You were trying to cling to me. It was horrible; you wouldn't let me go."

"I didn't have anyone but you, my fucking mother, that cold dark winters day you threw me to the wolves! I was your baby; your flesh and blood and you threw me, your baby to the wolves. And boy did they feast on me."

Now for the record, I've seen the sunny snaps with them both in nice locations. I was sitting on laps, all smiley, happy. So, what? who gives a fuck, I really don't care. I've seen pictures of Adolf Hitler with Eva Braun holidaying in the Austrian alps, but that doesn't change anything, does it now? He was still a first-class genocidal maniac. So those coastal glamping pictures, go fuck.

For the record this wasn't your typical abandonment, drop him off with this selfish, irresponsible fella. No. From what I've been told, he then took me to his current wife's house, whom he already had kids with. I believe it was somewhere in Scotland. He dropped me off like a dirty pair of knickers. I'm not her son; I'm the bastard he's just had with another woman behind her back. Why on earth would she want a bastard about the house? and she didn't, the abuse begins.

I was abandoned for years. Out there, Imagine that. Imagine being told that as a man with children of my own. The trauma alone as a baby is too much to bare. I've watched my son for hours, days, playing with his toys, being cheeky, and getting up to mischief, the lovable bundle of joy he is to us both and his big sister. It just doesn't compute that I could abandoned him, let alone our daughter. Wrap them up like a fish supper with a side order of mushy peas with pickled onions and leave them outside the YMCA. It just doesn't register anywhere.

I soon resigned my post in Birmingham. It didn't end well due to my mental state. I still regret how it ended, as some of my work colleagues were spot on. but my head was mangled. I couldn't bear to be within spitting distance of Doris, let alone that toxic, demented cunt of a woman—Phillis—who wanted me banished.

Fast-forward to 2020 a new decade. The previous three years were dreadful. Adíos; thank God that's over. Little did we know we would be slapped sideways with COVID-19. I mean, did God see that coming? Maybe. Did the chefs cooking up bat soup, pangolin stir fry with a side of crispy cats' ears and sweet and sour monkey chops? They should have. Wrong on all levels or is there something more sinister behind the pandemic? I mean what's more sinister than raping and burning the place we call home.

After the most horrific, lightning-speed psychotic meltdown driving home from work January 2020—and minutes away from ending my life on the M25 during rush hour—it was time for me to get some serious help. I needed serious help. I needed Gandalf the Grey and White. I needed Obi-wan Kenobi. I would have settled for Nurse Ratchet.

Over the course of treatment, I spoke with my elder sister and asked if we could talk about what she witnessed and if she knew about the abuse inflicted on me as a baby. So, we spoke. It crippled me, but I had to hear it, I needed to know if its was real, or all made up in my mangled head.

We spoke openly for about thirty minutes about general COVID-19 stuff before I dived in. She asked, "Are you sure you want to hear this?" Yes, I'm sure, I needed to know, I began. I do know I was abandoned for some time. During this time, Doris had moved up north from down south somewhere after divorcing Bob, the guy who thought I was his child when I popped out. Then she linked up with Boris. White dude, white woman Doris, back to Bobs surprise, maternity ward, out pops the wrong colour baby with an afro. They divorce because he can't bear the fact his wife has done the dirty and slept with a chap that had no place at Phillis's house. Yes, a darkie.

"I'm abandoned; we've done that part. But now I'm about to be bought back to Doris because I'm being seriously abused. Physically, verbally, emotionally battered. Now when I say, "seriously abused", I mean seriously abused. I'm finally reconnected with her and my sister—you—and the man who is going to make the next ten years of my life agonisingly painful, Boris. I'm rushed into the car. Doris is frantic, shouting to her new man, 'Get us out of here!' Sister is on the back seat, bonkers, screaming. Boris is also having a meltdown. I'm sure he's thinking, *What the fuck am I getting into? I've just hooked up with this broad, and I've inherited two fucking sprogs, one of them a halfbreed."*

Mother tore my jump suite off in a panic. I couldn't possibly imagine what my sister was going through, but she said I was covered in bruises and bite marks, battered, not in good shape, not in good shape at all. Looking at photos taken around that time, I would say I was no older than three. There are only two reasons I've surmised why I was in such a state. One, I was mauled by dog, due to my fear of dogs as a young boy. Or two, I was mauled by a human. Who, why, what, where, and when have never been explained to me. A baby passed from home to home, with no medical records or fixed abode, out there, for the sick pleasure of others.

A FRACTURED MIND

Soon as we enter the playground our little ones are off playing happily with the other children in the park. Two dark figures come in to focus wielding machetes. Before I could even move, one figure has mutilated several small children. The playground is a war zone, baby arms and legs strewn everywhere. A young mother has been decapitated by the other figure who then focuses on my little boy. Screams echo through my body, paralyzed, I can't do anything to prevent the carnage. "babe, babe, come on we have to leave the kids are hungry". I'm snapped out of another walking nightmare. Ok babe, I'm coming.

CHEESY SNACKS

Amsterdam to Germany, Germany to Amsterdam, early nighties. Before the big raid on military barracks across Germany after the Gulf War, to try and catch naughty soldiers like myself and band of druggie square heads, smuggling copious amounts of drugs into Germany as a squaddie was as easy as putting on a pair of drill boots.

I lost count of the trips I made to Amsterdam during my four-year posting, but it was a lot. The crazy thing is I didn't even have a driving licence. Imagine that, driving around Europe with no licence. Mental, proper mental. Talk about my head being somewhere else. But my military pass sufficed.

One evening me and a few chums made a last-minute dash for the 'Dam. The club named chocolate was the place to be; everything and anything was the norm there. I had been to a dozen gay clubs in Germany during the early nineties. Hardcore Frankie Goes to Hollywood with a dash of Priscilla, Queen of the Desert. All the gay clubs had the best DJs, music, and yes, the best drugs.

Itinerary: arrive Amsterdam, get smashed, procure drugs, get more smashed, go clubbing, get more smashed. Sleep in the car or smoke weed until we pass the fuck out. Wake up, public toilet, freshen up, breakfast, smoke weed, procure weed, solid and chemicals, coke, e's, PCP, speed and acid, and whatever else the goody-goody man is selling, pair of fake Ray Bons, maybe a beach towel. Don't mind if I do.

Smoke weed, begin the journey back to Germany. I've realised I'm carrying a load of olives and pickles—drugs—a lot more than I normally did. Panic doesn't set in as I'm peeled as a banana, up in smoke, dusted. Pit stop a few clicks from the border—toilet break, super-large coffee, mouthwash, munchies.

I purchase a family-size pack of cheesy puffs, a huge fucking bag, munchies, almost at the border we start to get restless, a tad, pockets full of delicious treats. The nutter on the back seat has a panic attack. "What if we get pulled over, and we get searched. I'm smashed, man, I'm really fucking smashed." Help me fella's, someone fucking help me.

"That will never happen, dude. We are squaddies." Universal soldiers, Jean Claude Van fucking Dam bollocks man.

"Fuck that, dude. There's no way I'm doing six months in a military prison, getting spit roasted by two hairy engineers. It just isn't going to happen." I'm a virgin man.

"What isn't going to happen, the get nicked part or you having your back doors smashed in by a hairy engineer?"

Okay, fuck it. Let's take no chances. So, I empty the all the cheesy puffs into my foot well. "Right, boys. Pass me all your stash. Hide what you can down your pants." I fill the empty bag with our side orders and top it off with cheesy puffs. I sling the rest out the window. Bosh, we are at the border.

Casual as a dog pissing on a lamp post, we pull the car up to immigration and show our military passes. Now, seen from a short distance, what I have in my hands is a bag of what appears to be cheesy puffs. And that's what I have, cheesy puffs. "gutten morgan mine frund, where are you traveling from?"

"Football game in Hengelo. Good game. Not too schabby." I offer the immigration officer my snacks. "Would you care for a cheesy puff?"

"Nine danka, I've just eaten mine frushstuck." Passes handed back to us, a nod, and we are free to go about our business. As we leave Amsterdam behind, to celebrate our juvenile ways, we all pop two tabs of acid, crank up the tunes and rave our way back to base.

Years later, after leaving the military, we all met at a rugby match in Twickenham. There was more cocaine being consumed that day than I've ever experienced. It was colossal. Walking around Tesco's, buying booze for the game, we did lines on top of display freezers. It was nuts, it was fucking pathetic. We spoke about the time we all dropped the two acid tabs. Looking back, we were never the same fellas after that trip to the 'Dam. Acid that strong, bonkers, proper bonkers, twitchy, twitchy eye syndrome.

Those who dance are considered mad by those who cannot hear the music, we were dancing and getting away with murder, I don't think anyone heard our tune.

POPPING OUT FOR A LOAF OF BREAD

When someone has a full blow addiction, it takes over. Procuring more drugs can be the main reason for getting out of bed in the afternoon. Much of the day is spent trying to think of ways to get more. I would do anything, absolutely anything to get out of the house to buy cocaine. I would pour all the milk down the sink, flush the bread down the toilet, make up all sort of bullshit to have an excuse. "Babe, I must go back to work, fire alarm has gone off, be back in thirty minutes." It would take at least an hour round trip to purchase the Bolivian, but fuck it, I needed it. I had to have it at all costs.

Friday night was a loaf of bread night once the little one went down. Out the door, brown or white babe and on my journey across town, I would literally be hyperventilating. My palms sweating, my balls tingling, and butterflies danced in my stomach (or maybe they were doing the pole vault). I was gagging for my fix.

When I finally arrived home, I didn't care about how many calls from my wife I had missed, let alone how to explain why I didn't have the loaf of bread I supposedly went out to buy. I got my fix and that's all I cared about. Cocaine was the love of my life, I didn't care if she cheated on me with millions of others, she gave me what I needed.

JERK CHICKEN WINGS

As far as irresponsible parents can push the boundaries of being irresponsible, sending your two children alone to parts of the United Kingdom on coaches to spend time with one's auntie and uncle, or in my sister's case, with her dad, is the premier league of irresponsibleness.

Before I continue, marching your children—eight and six years old—to the coach station and throwing them on a coach with a sandwich and a pound to Victoria Station from middle England is mad. When we arrived at Victoria, pockets full of random shit we stole from the service station, my sister would put me on my coach then head off to Cornwall. It doesn't happen today. It just doesn't happen. Back then it did, without a care in the world, off we went, so Boris and Doris could spend time together alone and with their new-born sons without two bastards about the house. I've thought about this endlessly over the years. Did they care for us? Well you're this far in the book, so you can guess the answer.

These shenanigans went on for years. Every half term from school and any other possible break, I'd be off. Bags packed, dumped on a coach, and sent to Ipswich. With regards to my sister, as mentioned, she was sent away to spend time with her biological father. Me? I was sent away for one specific reason, and that reason being I was an embarrassment and that bastard Boris didn't want me snivelling around the house all summer.

I'm no psychologist, and I don't have any experience whatsoever in psychology except for what I've experienced in being treated by psychologists and various doctors. But I believe this being sent away whenever possible, and everything else I was being subjected to, had a serious impact on me. I am, in fact, the manifestation of their neglect. So, what the fuck happened, what was happening around or above us. Was there some greater power at work here? Me and my sister could have easily been plucked from that coach by a paedophile, gagged in a dark cellar and ganged rape for weeks or until we bleed out.

A ticking time bomb started during my first unmanned mission to Ipswich at that tender age of 7. I began to lose all sense of who or what I was, where I was going, and why I was always being sent away. Basically, Doris wanted me out of her pathetic existence. But where did I belong? There was no father figure, no role model to look up to. There was no one I could call "Dad," Pops," "Father." There was only and always will be my auntie Stella. Regardless of how hardcore she was in her youth, she treated me like her own.

Doris never mentioned anything about my biological father, Johnny, until I was eleven, maybe twelve. What I remember from her failed attempt to explain I wasn't Boris's child went down like the titanic.

I really didn't give a fuck. I really didn't care what she was trying to say. I was beyond caring. I was a child who had been systematically broken-down month after month, year after year, by her and everyone who was a cunt. I was a victim of child abuse, relentless, non-stop abuse on all levels, Doris could have said my father was Father Christmas; it would not have made any difference.

Before I continue, I want to apologise to anyone reading this. If I could be more eloquent in explaining myself throughout this book, this project, I would. But I'm no Hunter S. Thompson or Bret Easton Ellis. I'm just me, trying to tell my story to the best of my ability. So please excuse me if this comes across as if it's been written by a dyslexic twelve-year-old who just turned forty.

Yes, where was I? Seemed to have gone around the houses there for a minute. That's it. I'm was starting to contemplate who I was, where was I from, Africa the Caribbean, any country where black people came from. I didn't know my heritage. I didn't have a clue, and

Doris didn't want to tell me. Doris didn't even know where he was from; no one did, only he did, and she didn't even know his proper name. So, I started thinking that I could have been adopted. I would have taken that on the chin any day. Maybe Doris adopted me, why wasn't anyone telling anything, or did I belong to someone else, knowing what I know now, it would not be a surprise me.

When I turned twenty-four, I met Johnny for the first time, totally random. No rush there then. The first question I asked was where the fuck he had been and where the fuck he was from. "I'm from Jamaica, son." Happy days, a rubber stamp on my forehead. "I'm from Jamaica." Finally, after spending two decades thinking I was from Barbados, I now have some form of Identity. I had just won countdown.

Where I belonged was a simple fact in my head—with my auntie Stella and her family. She was white. Her vivacious, charismatic, outgoing, handsome husband was black, and both their children— my cousins, my beautiful cousins—were the same colour as me, mixed race, dual heritage, half cast, toffee-caramel-brown. I fitted beautifully into the mix, so why wouldn't I call this home?

I had some sort of belonging. I truly felt part of the family; I *was* part of the family, and that Middle England only existed in my worst nightmares. But I'm fully aware it was not a nightmare; it was reality. From as young as I can remember, we did family things together with auntie Stella, my first life experiences. Good, healthy experiences happened in Ipswich. Everything was meaningful. I felt part of something. I felt free to be me without repercussions, or a slap for laughing out loud.

I can remember like it was yesterday spending long hot summers with my auntie Stella. She bought me and my cousins easy riders which provided access on all public transports across town. We travelled all over, visiting sports centres, parks, museums, outdoor swimming pools. Out all day, meeting friends and doing all the great stuff kids love to do. I had friends, not like the wankers I hung out with on that dreadful estate. Well maybe a few were okay, but the rest were wankers.

During the evenings, we hung out with other kids on the street, playing games, listening to music—Lose Ends was my favourite band during the eighties—and just generally had a good time. Returning home to Middle England a few days before school opened after the summer holidays was awful. I fucking hated it. Back to having my soul destroyed. The black kid within a family that within itself was, beyond doubt, proper fucked.

So here we go, and here it begins. In the most sarcastic of half-drunk voices, Doris asked, "What have you been up to all summer? Fuck all, I bet." Like she really cared. I mean really cared what I had been up to. It was her chance, her opportunity to ridicule me, embarrass me in front of everyone, and I mean everyone. And she loved it. Even my snivelling little half-siblings joined in.

Even if Phillis was or wasn't there, or if the neighbours happened to pop round for a drink, it was her sick and twisted sense of power over me. Toxic then and still toxic now. She even embarrassed me at my wedding. My wedding was her opportunity to spend time with her eldest daughter as opposed to spending time with me, my new wife, and her grandkids.

"Wedding day." "If it's okay, Auguste, I would like to sit and spend time with your sister as I don't see her often." Over the past 20 years Doris, has visited me twice, the second time being my wedding. My in-laws gave us £3,000 as a wedding gift. Doris, Alfred, and Phillis gave us £30. I didn't even bother to read the card because I know one of my half-siblings received twenty times that for his 3rd wedding, yes 3rd wedding gift. We would have settled for a bathmat.

I remember my auntie Stella and the gang enjoying jerk-style chicken wings for lunch one summer. I had never tasted anything like that before. Well what black kid would have tasted or heard of jerk spice growing up with the mashed potato and lumpy gravy soggy sprout family?

This was something new, something different. So, I told Doris, "5, 4, 3, 2, 1, lift off fucking chicken wings." It was like I had told the world's best joke. She laughed and laughed. "Chicken fucking wings. Have you fucking heard this you lot?" She was hysterical.

Every second word was, "fucking," and ended with, "chicken wings," or, "chicken wings fucking".

Imagine Oliver Twist receiving a beautiful roast chicken dinner, with all the trimmings, more trimmings than a Harvester salad bar. Could you imagine the look on his face? Could you imagine the smile he would have? Maybe his smile would be too big for his face. Well that was those chicken wings for me, and she fucking killed it.

TWO NIGGERS

Hey Auguste, what do you call two niggers in a sleeping bag? I don't know Sergeant, what do you call two of those you've just mentioned in a sleeping bag? A Twix, LOL do you get it, no sergeant I don't get it.

SOAP RAPED

My wife loves a bath. Me personally, unless I'm in a Turkish sauna eating baklava then it's showers all day long. Something in me just doesn't register when it comes to having a bath. Not even a well-deserved soak after a shift on the pans followed by service. Smelly candles, Barry White playing, bliss, no, not bliss, not for this kid.

I've mentioned already that everything was different for Boris. He got first-class treatment, he flew 1st class every day and we got what was left over, the scraps and on many occasions, his dirty bathwater to wash ourselves in before bed.

My auntie Stella hated Boris, absolutely hated him. She knew what was going on; she knew everything. My auntie always knew who my biological father was. I am baffled to this day that during all my summers in Ipswich, he was just down the road. Maybe it was him, maybe he didn't want nothing to do with me.

It was decided between Boris and Doris that I would have nothing to do with Johnny, my biological father. Boris would raise me as his own; that was the deal. I would be kept away from Johnny and wouldn't be told anything, not even his name, not his background, or where he was from.

Raise me as one of his own. Why would someone who painted my sister with black boot polish beat her with every kitchen utensil raise a half-breed as one of his own? I was kid growing up with no soul, no purpose, no direction, no ambitions, no one interested in my well-being apart from my auntie Stella, the phenomenal woman.

She could see the pain in my eyes, the hurt, but she couldn't do anything because Mother wanted it that way and forced my auntie not to say shit. My auntie could only give me the love, the same love she gave to her kids during my time with them. It was priceless. Its probably what kept me alive knowing the six-week school holidays we spent together and then the odd half-term break would recuperate me until I returned to no child's land.

Going way back, back to my first memories as a child, there is one memory that stands out, and its not a happy memory. Walking to school alone at the age of five or six was the norm. Well it was the norm for me because I don't remember any other kids walking alone.

Even at my pass-out parade from the army, I was the only soldier whose parents were absent. Totally embarrassed during the pass out reception, the only soldier making up excuses as why my, I'm going to hate saying this word "parents" where absent, and there I'm stood making up fucking excuses for them both. Good thing about the army, it gave me things I had never experienced before—belonging, three seriously good meals per day, structure, and the ability to believe in myself. The fights, the fascists, the racists wankers, the bumps and bruises, the scrapes I sustained during infantry training, my sergeant screaming down my ear every waking minute of the day wasn't anything I couldn't handle. Standard procedure for a kid dragged up on an estate called Pet Cemetery.

I remember walking home from school one grey cloudy day. It's mad because it always seemed grey in Middle England, always grey. I had soiled myself, a squelchy mess in my pants. I walked all the way home with my pants full of shit, breakfast and lunch; I was caked in it. Running down the insides of my legs, into my socks, I smelt like shit.

I arrived home. No hello, nothing like that. Boris had just finished an early shift. I know this because he was in the bath; it would have been around 3 p.m. The next thing I remember—and this is a memory clear as the driven snow I'm sitting in a bath of cold, dirty water. His dirty bath water covered in shit, covered head to toe in shit.

She left me there for the best part of an hour. By the time she pulled me from the swamp-infested, putrid bathwater, I must have had early systems of hypothermia and dysentery. I was wrapped in something resembling a towel and left in front of the coal fire, shaking uncontrollably.

Earlier I wrote that I don't do baths, and that is one reason. But there's another reason: soap. There were no fancy products back then, in that crumbling rat infested shit hole like you have today that I experienced. Soap made from whale flesh or whale oil is a smell you don't forget. It was most likely in every school back in the seventies and eighties, accompanied by tracing paper for bog roll. Wipe your ass, and it's halfway up your back.

Today I've heard it's good for you. "Great for your skin," they say. But it's not good for you if it is rammed up your ass. Not for a small child with constipation, not good at all. So, unless I am missing out on something here, maybe a Mr's Beeton's remedy in the good housekeeping guide in one of her many cookbooks for small children, then I guess it's some sort of twisted, medieval, Wicked-Witch-of-the-West thing to do.

Constipation is caused by a poor diet with not enough fibre, fruit, vegetables or eating too much cardboard. Knowing today how twisted and tormented Doris and her mother were and are, it most likely started with a phone call to SS headquarters from the pay phone on the corner of the street.

"He's been constipated for a while now. What do you suggest?" Doris is having a confab with the SS leader who didn't want me anywhere near her gestapo bunker when Doris first took me there.

"Constipation is it?" Nanny Phillis is most likely thinking, *what sick and twisted remedy can I conjure up?* Bingo! "Have you tried inserting a bar of soap up his bum?" Now why didn't Doris consult with our GP or take me to A&E if it was that bad, a child laxative, or maybe a telephone conversation with someone less twisted, like my auntie.

The smallest slightest incident or thing can trigger a flashback which can transport you back to that very moment. You don't have to believe it, it's true. What triggers this memory, is a bath, a fucking bath. I'm led into the bathroom. The bath was downstairs, near the kitchen. I remember because the radio was on, and the radio was always kept in the kitchen. Until one-time 'King Kong' Boris launched it up the garden, kind of a radio vacation outdoors for the electrical device.

The pain was excruciating, more painful than any hiding I had experienced, white pain. As a bit of a plonker, in my late twenties and early thirties, anyone who knew me, knew I was mad for snowboarding, aka the astronaut, with such an extreme sport, that I loved, come consequences, such as concussions, sprains, broken bones, and in extreme cases, death.

If you've broken a collarbone, you'll know what white pain is. It's decapitation with your head still attached to your body. Not for kids. It stung, it stung so bad it felt like I had a dozen hornets in my arse. Tears poured from my eyes, but I was unable to make a sound as I had lost my breath. I had rigor mortis; I was being soap raped. This wasn't some old housewife's remedy for constipation. This was torture at the highest level. A nice soak in the bath after a hard day's work listening to my favourite eighties band playing in the background, nice smelly candles, you can fuck right off.

The odd thing was, for several days after this back breaking, monstrosity of a soap raping, every time I farted, several bubbles came out my baby bottom.

RACISTS EVERYWHERE

Even at the highest levels of management, executive
management, there are racists, its just another thing
we must deal with when we are at the top.
"Fuck me chef does like to talk after a few beers and a bottle
of vino, I know throw a banana at him see what happens".
You're an absolute wanker, I wouldn't have expected that from
GM. I would have expected more from you, but its obvious
you have a big mouth and are in fact a racist wanker. "What's
happened guys"? Why has chef left the table? "Someone,
I will not say who, wanted to throw a banana at him".

WELCOME TO THE WORLD OF COOKING PART 1: A CHEF'S INTRODUCTION.

I t's not the easiest thing, adapting to the outside world when you've had the wind constantly knocked out of your sails for the past decade. "Wipe that smile off your face, or I'll wipe it off for you." "Why are you so fucking happy?" "If you don't stop crying, I'll give you something to cry for."

So, in a nutshell, was I ready for the outside world? No, I wasn't. I had been enrolled at college at a young age; 15, it was just how my birthday fell in the year. During the first year of college, all students had to complete a two-week work experience placement as part of our studies to experience life or death in a working kitchen.

My work experience was at the prestigious four-star Opera Hotel in town. Every celebrity who stared in any pantomime in town stayed there during the eighties, and probably still do. I was mad nervous, proper nervous. I was doing well at my studies, practical and theory. When you made a good stock or sauce, or trussed a bird ready for the pot, you received good praise from your tutor. The more praise I got, the harder I worked. The harder I worked, the better my craft, and with that, my confidence started to grow.

Just a short detour if I may: I know I swear from time to time. Some may say I swear because of a poor education. No, the education wasn't poor; I just didn't get it. With my bullshit homelife, how the fuck could I concentrate at school not knowing what was in store for me when I got home or the mood of the household. It was play your cards right every other day. So, finding something I was good at and enjoyed meant a lot, it meant everything.

Besides, if anyone's ever accused you of sounding less intelligent because you swear too much, don't worry. A study found that those who have a healthy repertoire of curse words at their disposal are more likely to have a richer vocabulary than those who don't. Fucking great cut and paste.

My first shift began at eight Monday morning. I had all weekend to get prepared. I pressed my whites and sharpened my knives. I can't remember the specific dates, like a lot of things today, but this work experience in the winter of 1986 was going to be a game changer.

Monday morning, I was up early. I brushed my teeth, sprayed my pits, grabbed my clobber, and was out the door. No, "Good luck son," or anything like that. They knew it was only a matter of time before I was going to leave anyway and get out of their miserable lives.

What the hell was a, "Good luck, son," going to do for me anyway? This work experience would either make me or break me. Break me, and my future would have been so much more different. Wanting to prove my family and every scumbag who wanted to see me fail was my doing. It was going to be my ultimate addiction in proving my entire family wrong. An addiction where by I would attempt to take my life.

This is where my mind begins to wonder as I reminisce at the life I've managed to forge for myself, I can only smile. The guys I used to look up to, had the cool gear, the bikes, the family stand. Even the local shoplifter's, and the dead beats uptown were cool. The guys who would fight on Bond Street outside pubs and clubs on a Friday or Saturday night I thought they were so cool.

In fact, I thought every reprobate around town during the eighties was cool, probably because they were in their moment at that given time. I, however, was that lost soul who hadn't a clue where the fuck he was going. I just followed them, half the time getting up to no good. I started shoplifting, stealing bikes, stealing people's luggage off trains. If I thought I could steal it, I'd have it, and I didn't even consider the consequences.

I stole a bag off a train once with two other losers from a train station in Middle England. We were chased by the British transport police. So where do we run? Through a mile-long tunnel out of the station. We shut down the entire train service in the West Midlands for two hours. What dickheads. If we had fallen on the tracks, electrocuted, we'd be dead, hit by a Thomas the tank engine, the obvious.

It's a million miles away and a million reasons how I made it. Someone upstairs must have known a child born into so much carnage, and destruction might deserve an opportunity in life. I suppose it's why I use the phrase, "Kissed by God." Am I religious? Yes, but you'll never see me wearing sandals and socks.

I jumped on the bus, headed into town, I entered the kitchen via the staff entrance. This instruction was on my brief from the college's "First Day on the Job, back doors", I was greeted by the executive chef

"Change in my office. I'll be back in five to show you the ins and outs of my domain," he instructed me. The office consisted of a wooden table and chair, an ash tray, twenty B&H, half a bottle of whisky, dirty coffee cups, rizla, dirty chef whites on the floor, and a poster of Sam Fox pinned to the wall, tits out of course.

Starters, mains, pastry, pot wash, fridges, fire exit, my office. My first job was to prep broccoli for a function. Wasn't told which function, just to prep. I was dwarfed by six crates of broccoli. *No sweat. Let's crack on. Florets in the container, stalks in the bin,* I thought.

I practically stood outside as the prep area was situated to the rear of the kitchen, near the back doors. Within the hour, I was done, I cleaned my section and emptied the bin.

Now I didn't think anything of prepping the broccoli that quickly, neither throwing out the stalks, I just did it. A few more chefs arrived on shift and I was whisked around the kitchen during lunch service. I'm in my element, or so I thought.

The executive chef screamed across the kitchen, "Where the fuck are the broccoli stalks?"

Broccoli stalks, "Chef, I threw them out, the florets are in the prep fridge." Ever see a silverback ape on PCP? Yeah, a silverback ape on PCP with an erection. Well that's what this chef had turned into, chef Ramsey hasn't got shit on this chef.

If he'd said, "Stalks in that container," then I would have done the obvious. Now I thought the verbal abuse at home was bad, but this was on another level, another level on top of mount Everest level.

In-my-face, mustard-in-the-eye-sockets petrified, the ape on PCP with his lipstick poking out of his chef's trousers was going off. "Fuckin' bin. Get your black fuck ass out there, and get me those fucking broccoli stalks you fucking, spellcheck, gollywog." *Humm, gollywog,* I thought correct. "Get out there and fetch me those stalks you black twat".

The day had turned to a bleak winter's afternoon. Artic winds swirled around bins the size of a garden sheds. No recycling back in those days. Every department just dumped their shit in any bin. "Get in those fucking bins and get me those broccoli stalks."

"Oui, chef, yes chef".

Into the bin I go, full chef's whites—apron, hat, neckerchief, and so on. Within minutes I was frozen to the bone; believe me, there wasn't much meat on me back in those days. Knee-deep in hotel waste, the smell was something else. I ripped bags apart, throwing out every stalk.

Before long, I was back in the kitchen a total mess. The broccoli stalks were covered in all sorts of detritus. "Good lad. Now get them washed and bring them to me in the sauce section when you're ready."

"Yes chef, oui chef, yes chef, yes oui chef"

That evening on the menu, cream of broccoli and blue cheese soup topped with garlic-herb croutons, finished with creme fries, and garnished with the classic eighties' garnish chopped parsley. At 6 p.m. I was told to fuck off home and come back tomorrow if I dared. I cried all the way home, destroyed, beaten black and blue, wounded, broken. Fuck this chef malarkey for a living I thought.

I arrive home battered. I smelt bad, proper nasty, hotel waste nasty. There was no sympathy. Why would there be? Snivelling like a child lost in Woolworths, I attempted to explain my day. "I can't go back there. This cooking thing is not for me."

"You better get your fucking ass back there tomorrow or else."

That's the day my future as a chef was set in stone. Those words, "You better get back there or else," was the only piece of encouragement I needed to get me out of that God-forsaken house.

First job the following morning was to melt chocolate and make garnishes for the pastry chef. Nuclear-powered microwave no problem, chocolate in two minutes. Not good, not good at all, black chocolate toxic smoke covered half the entire kitchen. Chefs and waiter's half choked to death, it couldn't get any worse. I went back every day for two weeks regardless, battered, broken, shattered, mentally and physically exhausted.

This chef was a lunatic, don't like my racist remarks? Go fuck yourself. Fuck, shit, crap wank, go fuck yourself. HR go fuck yourself some more." Human resources back then: "Go fuck yourself." Is this how all chefs acted, "go fuck yourself", in fact if you don't like it, go be something fucking else, and while you're at it, go fuck yourself.

•

THE MILLION-DOLLAR QUESTION

"Auguste, where do you see yourself in 5 years"? Well my career goal, to be an executive chef within a prestigious 5* hotel, like this beautiful establishment, with a Michelin starred restaurant in my name. I mean really, how the fuck was I going to achieve all that, being the maddest frog in a bag of a dozen crazier frogs. My skills set was on point, I had worked 2 & 3 Michelin stars but besides being a functioning maniac with the mentality of an anorexic caveman the only kid in the room I was kidding, was me.

WELCOME TO THE WORLD OF COOKING PART 2: THE DANCING CHEF

The bus journey to the restaurant was a good forty-five minutes if I caught the connecting bus from the depot. If I didn't, I was screwed, a two-hour walk. The fare wasn't a problem. In those days I had my bus pass, a freebie for all those on a welfare while at college.

The Jockey Club was a funky, renowned establishment that catered for the in-crowd on the outskirts of town. Big wigs, footballers, celebrities you name it. Winter 1987, it was going to be my second work experience from college.

I had the basic skills in my locker: bread making, classic cuts of vegetables—paysanne, brunoise, and julienne, as well as macedoine and jardinière—and butchery of all the basic meats and filleting fish. I knew the basic sauces and their derivatives, Françaises, cake making, pastry, waiting tables, and basic sommelier skills in all good City and Guilds fashion. It was time to jump back in and experience the world of hospitality again.

Up, washed, porridge, college-issued chefs' whites in my happy shopper bag. Unlike the endless selection we have today, once you washed your whites, they'd shrink. And if they had creases, they were fucked; a steam roller couldn't get them out.

I had my chefs' knives, college issued, wrapped in a tea towel–type binder made of the same material your jacket was made from. There were inserts for peelers, Parisienne cutters, a huge chef's knife, a filleting knife, and a boning knife.

I had a serrated knife for carving up work benches and bread, a turning knife and a steal which was as much use as a blunt spoon once you'd chopped the tops of your fingers clean off. But they were free, and they were my tools.

Of course, I had the *Repertoire De Cuisine*. You had to buy it out of your own pocket, but it cost peanuts compared to what it is worth today; it's a collector's item. I still have mine, under lock and key mind you, stuck together with masking tape and covered in every sauce I made during my college years. Any chef from that era must have one lying around somewhere.

I was out the door and off to the Jockey Club, I arrived twenty minutes early. I assumed it would be a good sign for whoever was going to show me the ropes for the next two weeks. "Good morning. My name is Auguste."

"Go fuck yourself. Only joking. I know who you are."

"I'm here for my two weeks' placement."

"Not another one", the receptionist mutters under her breath. "Sit over there. I'll call the kitchen and let them know you're here."

Another what? I pondered. *A cheese-grating wanker?*

There was a certain smell about the place, like a damp storage cupboard. There was carpet everywhere, on the walls, ceilings, downstairs, and up the stairs leading to what I guessed were guestrooms.

"Are you Auguste?"

"Yes, that's me."

"We've been expecting you. You're late." She must have heard my insides fall out my arse. First day at work and late. "Jesus! Only messing with you. You're early, silly twat. Come on. I'll show you where to get changed."

I followed the chef up the stairs and through a maze of twisted low-ceiling corridors. "Here we go, a toilet." I could have gotten changed outside in the snow for what it was worth. "Get changed and come down to the kitchen."

"Yes chef. Oui chef."

"Mr Conte is off this morning. He'll be in this evening, so it's me and you, chicken. We have a party tonight for 120."

"Who's Mr Conte."

"He's the head chef and co-owner. Okay, hot section, larder which doubles up for desserts, cold room, and out back, across the car park, dry stores."

"Cool, cool."

"Your first job is preparing chickens. Follow me."

I grasped my blunt set of knives and was led down a flight of stairs and into a room that seemed like a torture chamber. Hooks hung from the ceiling. There was one flickering light bulb minus the cover, a wooden butcher's block covered in salt, a leaking sink, and stacks of crates full of chickens.

It was fucking freezing, Baltic. Oh, and I forgot the two kitchen porters locked in a bamboo cage in the corner. Talk about hell's kitchen. This was it.

"Here we go, butchery section." Butchery? What section? are you kidding me. "You know how to prepare a chicken for sauté, don't you?"

"Yeah." Qui chef.

"Cool beans. Give me a shout if you need anything. I'll be in a nice warm kitchen doing shit for tonight."

"A duffle coat and some gloves maybe."

"Ha, ha. You're funny. Chop, chop."

Sudden thoughts of doing a runner out the back door seemed an option "Do legs, get the fuck out of here," *Apocalypse Now* raced through my head. But where to? Home? I don't think so. I was obsessed, addicted in getting out of that place.

I was down there for what seemed like eternity, hacking and chopping at these poor dead creatures. But it wasn't with the lack of knowing where to chop, where to slice, and what parts to hack off. I knew these fellas inside out—poultry half, breast quarter, leg quarter, leg, drumstick, thigh, wing, flat wing tip, two bone. The carcasses were used for stock. Halfway through the stack of crates, I started playing around, cutting up chickens with my eyes closed, popping out the thigh bone from the under-carcasses with a snap of my wrist. It wasn't so bad after all.

All the time I was down there, my mind was free, free of all issues, my childhood, my purpose in life, my identity, I hadn't thought about anything, not a single thing but my sixty new friends who hadn't been slaughtered in vain. They were going to be something special—coq au vin—for tonight's function and enjoyed by many.

When I went to take a piss, I had to sit down because my dick had shrivelled inwards due to the extreme cold. My hands were blue, my feet, blocks of ice, and my eyebrows iced over. "You all right down there, chicken? How you are doing for time."

"I'm fine thanks. Almost done." Almost done, and it wasn't even lunchtime.

Split shifts were all the go back in those days. You were lucky if you got out. I spent my first split shift sitting in the toilet cubical, ironically eating chicken and chips cooked by my new nemesis. After I finished, I just sat there wondering if I could get away with a quick wank.

Four bells and back in the kitchen. I wandered down to the slaughterhouse to check on my birds. The man himself—Mr Conte, head chef and co-owner of the Jockey Club—was already there, inspecting my work. He was fucking huge. I mean Andre the Giant huge. He didn't don the classic checked trousers and the jacket made of rhino skin. Oh no. He wore Ron Hill joggers, Fruit of the Loom T-shirt, Hi Tec trainers, and a butcher's apron.

"Is this your work?"

"Yes, chef."

"Did that lesbian give you a hand?"

"No, chef."

"Did you cut yourself?"

"No, chef."

"Where are you from?"

"Fire town chef, the other side of town, chef."

"Do you suck dick?"

"No, chef."

"Follow me."

He led me back into the kitchen, his stage, so to speak, where he dazzled many with his delights. I got a funny feeling that he had taken a liking to me, probably because I didn't suck dick. What if I did suck dick? Would that be a problem?

Maybe he liked my chicken chopping skills. It wasn't any of those. Mr Conte was a people person who enjoyed working with young chefs delving into his world. He wasn't a chef like you hear about today, a load of pan-throwing lunatics off camera. He was the coolest person I had ever meet, unlike those wankers I was knocking about with over the weekends.

He liked to show off his skills. He was a showman, and that night he made me sit and watch him dance around the kitchen for the entire service. This huge Italian chef singing, cooking, joking with the waiting staff without a care in the world—apart from his cooking, and he cooked well, really fucking well.

The following weeks we prepared game and offal, food I saw at the markets in town many years while shopping for the household, fodder for the weekend. The freshest of produce turned into beautiful, wholesome, delightful dishes. We cooked sole Colbert, sole Veronique, whitebait with lemon wedges, tournedos Rossini, steak Dian, steak tartar, T-bones and rib eyes, spatchcocked chicken. I lost count of the pasta dishes he cooked with what sauces and types of pasta.

I made potted shrimps and salmon roulade with the dodgy-looking female chef. Even she was a legend, she didn't care where you were from, what tribe you belonged to, your religion, or sexual orientation. There was something about her in those chefs' whites, something very attractive. The fact she could cook like Mr Conte was what was attractive. I indulged in all aspects of the kitchen, dressing the dessert trolley for the evening service, scooping out pineapples and filling the shells with the pulp and Chantilly cream, making all sort of gateaux's garnished with so many types of fruits and berries.

There was papaya, physalis, star fruit—the most astrological fruit of them all—mint sprigs, berries, toasted coconut and almonds, chocolate shavings, vermicelli, and glace cherries. There was nothing fancy about Mr Chef Conte, nothing complicated. Everything he did was done with simplicity, in fresh, cooked classic, garnished well, and served to the salivating customers.

He was the greatest chef I ever learnt from. My time spent with Mr Chef Conte for those two weeks was a time I'll never forget. A huge gentleman of a chef who took me under his wing and made sure my journey through his kitchen was one of joy and happiness. Fuck knows what happened after that. Must have been the war.

I returned to college two weeks later mad for it. As happy as a free-range organic chicken. I was like a pig in shit. I was hooked, buzzed out; nothing fazed me. I studied my repertoire inside out, back to front, day in and day out. I tested myself on the thousands of recipes, picking up kitchen French along the way, preparing myself for the real world.

City and Guilds 7061 & 2 French classical cookery, passed. Patisserie and baking passed. Food and beverage service for the hospitality industry passed. Culinary French terminology, all over it like a rat on a Big Mac.

DEMENTIA PLUM CRUMBLE

Hands down, if I'm playing a game of dice or cards today, the hand of all hands is going to be a full house, sprouts over plum crumble. I have no love in the world for tinned plums as I do sprouts, no love whatsoever. Bullet to the head or tinned plum crumble, bullet to the head, skin peeled from my body with a blunt spoon, or tinned plum crumble, the skin-peeling thing. Molested by a giraffe over plum crumble, the molesting thing.

"Okay, kids, it's off to your grandparents." Not my grandparents, fascists. "She's made her lovely crumble for us all. What a treat." I had two fingers to the back of my throat already retching before we've made it to the car for the journey across town for dog shit dementia crumble with cold, lumpy, fox-vomit custard.

No disrespect, but she isn't no Italian granny chef. The crumble topping resembled the glue you used at infant school to stick fairy liquid bottles together with green garden sticks to make a sail and gravel for sand. Yes, warm, gravel-type burnt topping with the gluey glop between that and the filling.

The whole dish was presented like a Joel Robuchon masterpiece in a battered Pyrex dish. We all had to marvel at it and then sit there and consume it like it was a warm, triple-chocolate fudge cake, with more fudge on top of the fudge, caramel filling with vanilla bean ice cream and marshmallows, and then fudge sauce poured on top. Garnished, of course, with sprinkles and chocolate wafers.

Fuck that shit. I was more than prepared to be at the table for two weeks. I knew Phillis didn't have a shotgun, so what was the worst that could happen, I don't get a blue ribbon for being a good boy because I didn't eat all my pudding? You can stick that blue ribbon where the sun has never shined. I'm a soldier in the making and you or your crumble will not break me.

WHEN MENTAL HEALTH SAID HELLO

The first-time mental health said hello to me, it was 2007. I was out in Australia with my ex-partner. Her parents had given us their holiday home for the week. It was a three-hour drive north of Sydney, in a small collection of exclusive chalets within a private gated area. The place was stunning. Her parents' chalet was proper bling, spacious, well stocked, all the "mod cons".

The first evening we settled in, BBQ and drinks, the following morning we walked to the local seaside resort which was no bigger than a small village, beautiful. It was no stroll up the garden pathway and a gentle knock at the door when mental health introduced itself to me. No, no, no.

It was violent, like a dozen bullets to the head, an axe to the face, a shovel up my ass, a skewer up my nose, boiling sugar poured over my ball sack, my spin pulled from my body via my ears. We had just walked out of a beautiful souvenir shop, and *bang!* The big bang went off like lemon juice and salt on the brain.

Anger, horror, murder, violence, rape, genocide, mutilation ran through my veins. I wanted to kill everyone in sight. I had visions of myself walking through that village and killing everything and everyone. Women, children, old folk, any who moved. I had guns, knives, machetes, the whole fucking shcbang playing out like some fucking horror movie while I'm walking hand in hand with my partner. "You okay, babe?"

"Yeah, I'm fine, babe." Fine? How far from the fucking truth, what was I going to say? That I'm the grim reaper on speed? Fine was me in a silk bathrobe, wearing fluffy slippers, sipping a nice glass wine eating smelly cheese watching a sci-fi movie.

This played out for the best part of two hours. Lemon juice in my eyes, nails in my brain, scotch bonnets lodged in the back of my throat. I was fucking drowning. I didn't know what to do, what was going on. I was scared, frightened. It was the first time I felt the presence of the cold, dark blanket—suicide. Killing myself would have been the easy option that day. Back to the villa, rusty box cutter across the wrists and throat, job done.

I'd just been brain raped, and it didn't feel good. The only way I was going to suppress this was with booze, loads of booze, until I passed the fuck out. Several weeks later welcome home United Kingdom, dealer, drugs, booze. I hid away for several days, several fucking days in a drug induced self-medicating coma.

Hello, it's me again, "MH2", Christmas 2009. I'm driving to Ipswich to be with my cousins, and it was the first time my future wife would meet my family.

Christmas Day, It's crisp and fresh outside, blue skies, picture perfect. I walked into the kitchen pumped for our Christmas breakfast. I pictured myself smashing my now-wife's face into the sink and cutting her head off with a carving knife. I sliced off both her breasts and volleyed her head through the window.

Yet again out of the fucking blue, *boom!* Scrambled brain and smoked salmon for breakfast. I saw myself sitting at the table and hacking at my cousin's throat with a blunt dinner knife, attacking it like some ravaged cannibal, writing "Merry Crimbo" on the table with her warm blood. I've cooked the little one in the microwave and hanged everyone else from the Christmas tree, there was peeled flesh covered in marmite and sprinkles hanging from the ceiling, on with dinner preparations.

Please, God, this can't be happening, what is going on, I've just entered the gates of hell on Christmas Day and my head was screaming from the inside. Black and grey shadows shrouded my racing thoughts. *Why am I having these thoughts, thoughts about*

57

hurting my loved ones, hurting the ones I love? I was well and truly messed up. "Messed up" is putting it lightly considering my mindset.

It being Christmas, the only way to deal with this was to drink and drink I did, I drank like 10 men in Weatherspoon's. When breakfast was over, I put on my chef's jacket on and began prep. I had three large glasses of wine positioned around the kitchen in case I forgot where I had put one. Plus, a can of beer was open in the fridge, and there were the standard 30-minute vodka shots. When dinner had finished, I would be upstairs chopping out a fat lines of cocaine, which would just accelerate everything and make the thoughts inside my head triple worse, more booze, more hard booze and more cocaine was the answer. If I couldn't snort it, id fucking smoke it. If I couldn't smoke or snort it, Id eat it.

After years of self-inflicted abuse, I could handle my booze and drugs. LOL. Sorry, hold on. Handle my booze and drugs? No, the booze and drugs were handling me. When I came down from a session, my thoughts were on another level. I'd have thoughts and visions of walking to the local train station in the village, a five-minute walk from our house, and stepping out in front of the first train to Paddington.

Flying was a nightmare. I believed I had Goliath strength and could take down anyone, even a plane filled with passengers. I would casually stroll to the door, look around, pretend to stretch and yawn, and then make a mad scramble to open it. Fucking chairs, people, trolley dollies were sucked out. Then I would snap out of it, distracted by something, I would order several small plastic bottles of wine.

I mutilated my wife a hundred ways, I slaughtered all my neighbours in the most horrific ways. Burnt my friends alive, suffocated my daughter, and raped and murdered countless victims. I decapitated more people than I can remember, I chopped up and buried countless victims. The more aggressive and violent the thoughts, the more drugs and alcohol I consumed. The more I consumed, the stronger the comedowns which resulted in attempted suicide.

I wasn't only addicted to drugs and alcohol. I was also addicted to sex, porn, strip clubs, the whole fucking buffet. I wanted it all, and I took it all. Every fucking piece of an intoxicated boozy brunch in Dubai; I smashed the lot. To this day I cringe, I cringe at some of things I did and some of the situations I put myself in during those horrific episodes of total and utter madness.

To this day I haven't had the stomach to tell anyone—my wife, family members, closest friends, let alone psychologists or any of the doctors I have recently had assessments with—about the actual thoughts I was having for fear of being sectioned or considered a risk. Please forgive me if what you are reading has bought tears to your eyes, but these visions were the awake versions of my nightmares.

"But"—and this is no ordinary "but"—all my thoughts, thank God and heaven on earth and all above, everything I was thinking was passive. The slightest thought that I was in a physical state to commit any such acts of horror towards anyone, my life would have been the price, quick easy and painless, first train to Paddington.

What I remember most about those times I sat with my physiologist or doctor during one of the many visits to A&E for overdosing ... By the way, there is a banging rave tune from the early nineties called "Overdose": It goes something like this: "Mr Smith your son is dead, how did he die, he died of an overdose," then the most insane break beat.

Apologies totally went off road there again. Let's try and remain focused as I would like to finish this project. Yes, my childhood always come up as pieces of the puzzle. The subject somehow, somewhere always came up, my childhood, I was in no state to put two and two together. How could I possibly put to and two together if two and two equalled 4 tickets, more drugs.

I remember I once said to Doris at a family birthday—I think it was hers—that I had problems with cocaine. She looked at me like a gold fish and said, "Sorry, son, that was never my thing" and walked off. Not a solitary member of that god forsaken family wanted to know my sickness. They would change the subject and empathize at a toxic level that sexual predators within the family were somewhat misunderstood. If I could write words down that could describe the disgust I have, "CUNTS".

All they wanted was to cling to me like leeches, like blood-sucking swamp leeches, so that maybe I would become one of them. A father with too many kids to mention, a parent who would do nothing and watch his flesh and blood beaten by other people. That somehow, I would continue the abuse that was a part of their heritage for decades before me. Well it didn't turn out that way, fuckers.

MIGUEL'S TOYS

**There is nothing in this godforsaken house
and no child needs nothing**

During the early years with Boris and Doris, my sister and I lived in absolute fear. I was just a child, but this was the age I really started to remember things. I can close my eyes as a man today and go back to how shit life was then, living in fear day in day out, not knowing what was in store for us pesky kids.

"Quick, kids," she would shout as Boris pulled onto the driveway. Well it wasn't a drive as such, just the front garden. "Your dad's home," she would shout, and we would literally run for cover. We would hide under tables, beds, in cupboards, anywhere we thought we were safe. Anywhere we could hide we'd fucking hide, and Mother would make it a hundred times worse. "Quick, kids, he's coming. Quickly go and hide before he sees you." This wasn't playful shenanigans. This was her putting the fear of God in us.

We scampered, terrorized, our little hearts beating out of our little chests. "Quick, he's at the door." The only reason I can come up with for this kind of terror—well, there are probably a dozen—but the main one being that she totally fucking resented the air we breathed, the ground we walked on; she felt total resentment toward us. The sheer sound of those footsteps walking through the house still sends shivers down my spine.

The love I have for my son & daughter is breath-taking. Every waking hour they remind me of all the beauty in the world. They remind me why I must be better and overcome my demons. *Love* is what defines us. *Love* is what holds our family together. It's what I try to embrace every day, regardless of whether it's a good or bad day.

I never felt the slightest ounce of love as a child growing up in that God-forsaken house. Every day was filled with screaming, domestic abuse, fights between her and him. Every day was misery, the house was infested with mice and rats running freely during the night. I could hear them scratching around beneath my bed. It was vile, damp, and depressing. Maybe we were the rodents living in their house.

The garden was always overgrown. There were trees at the bottom, we often built dens, me and my sister. There was also a waste ground through and beyond the fence at the bottom of the garden. There were slag heaps of old building sites, weeds, and boulders. During the summer, wild mint miraculously grew. As a chef, my favourite herb is mint. If I'm having a bad day at work, I walk into the vegetable fridge, grab a bunch of mint, hold it to my nose, and take a deep breath. It takes me back to the only time I found some sort of normality, scratching around on the wasteland at the back of our crumbling house, tearing at the wild mint, holding it to my young nose, and smelling something beautiful.

Most weekends, Boris and Doris left us to fend for ourselves while they went out. My sister would have been no older than seven; I would have been about five. Mother would put their firstborn as a couple to bed, eighteen months young at a push, and leave my sister and me to it.

This is how they rolled. They'd fuck off out without a care in the world, leaving two vulnerable children and a baby alone. As adults, my sister told me how, at the age of seven, she tried to deal with the baby's night terrors. Imagine that, a seven-year-old looking after me and an eighteen-month-old baby who brought the house down with night terrors.

It really hasn't been easy writing this. I've been tapping away on my keypad words, sentences flowing for the past few days, and I'm feeling physically sick remembering the neglect. My sister would panic, and the only option would be to bang on the neighbour's door, screaming crying, traumatised, asking for help.

"Where's your mom and dad?" the neighbour would ask. "They've left us. They went out," my sister would tell the neighbour. It was neglect on a scale that would have parents banged away today, well maybe not.

When Boris and Doris finally arrived home, they would be intoxicated. We would be punished for not dealing with baby. We'd be smacked about and told we were useless. "Useless fucking kids you are, fuck knows why I had you fucking pair, fucking waste of space."

There wasn't one night when I was a kid that I didn't cry myself to sleep. I cried out the pain as I shivered in a cold bed under an itchy blanket. There was no heating through the house, except for a shitty little coal fire downstairs. I cried until the world I was living in finally disappeared until woken by the sheer cold.

Some nights I would wake up due to the noise of the mice scratching under my bed. I remember vividly to this day I would get out of my bed with just my pants on, walk along the landing to mother's room, crawl under her bed and fall asleep on the floor. I was too scared to climb into her bed and ask for attention and warmth.

There were nights I woke up and the side of my face felt like it was burning, as if someone had slapped me in the face. I would be too scared to move an inch. I would be frozen in time, staring at the figure in the doorway to my room. I fucking knew it was him; I just knew. The fucking coward not only was it enough to be fucked over while awake, this abuse was going on while I was asleep. You're a cold-hearted bastard.

Back then, when I had knobbly knees and wore nothing but pants and a T-shirt around the house, I can't recall ever playing with toys. Our 'toys' were bricks and sticks. The one time I did have a toy was Christmas circa 1976. I was given a train set, a single track with an engine pulling a carriage around in a circle. I played with my Christmas present once, that same day, it disappeared.

The following Christmas, I got the same train set. The batteries must have leaked in the box throughout the year because there was silver foil crammed into where the batteries sat. It didn't even work.

A had a friend, Miguel, who lived a few doors up from us. I haven't a clue how we started hanging out together, most likely his mother babysat me. My friend had some amazing toys, including a figure of eight Scalextric, so many types of cars with a garage, and action men with vehicles. It was like Santa's grotto.

I truly loved being at Miguel's house, playing for hours on end in his bedroom. It was *Toy Story* personified. This is the first time I remember my first beating. I know there were others before this, but this was the first one I remember in my little brain. I always made my own way back and forth to Miguel's house. I arrived home after an awesome afternoon at his house, smiling from ear to ear, my face beaming as I walked into the house. "What the fuck are you smiling for? You better wipe that smile off your face before your dad sees you." Fucking dad. Hitler more like. The fucking audacity to call him my dad. He was a bully who preyed on me and my sister.

He walked into the living room, stood next to Doris, and asked why I was smiling and so cheerful. She asked me, "Did you have a nice time?"

"Yes, I loved it. He's got so many toys. We played and drank squash. It was awesome."

She asked in a sarcastic tone, "Would you like to live with your friend?"

"Yes. Just because he has nice toys."

"Well, you've asked for it now." I was dragged upstairs by that man. I was stripped naked and beaten, fucking beaten. My sister could hear my screams and cries for help in the garden. Doris was nowhere to be seen. That evil woman didn't raise a finger to protect me; she stood by and let it all happen. Raise me as one of his own? It makes me laugh out loud today. "One of his own"—the hatred that filled that dungeon was like a 2nd world war concentration camp.

A week later I was back at Miguel's house. I strolled down the road on my way home, wearing a gleaming smile. I'm convinced they were waiting for me because as I entered the house, I was summoned to the kitchen and asked the same question.

My answer was the same. Yes, I would love to live with my friend. Boris told me to go upstairs and strip naked. My sister was in the kitchen, kicking, yelling, screaming, "Don't you touch him. Don't you lay a finger on him, or else I will run away." This went on for some time. I could clearly hear my sister desperately pleading with Doris to help me.

While my sister was pleading with her, upstairs I cowered behind the door in my pants, petrified, shaking, whimpering. I knew only one thing: I was minutes away from another beating. But he never came upstairs that afternoon. My sister had saved me. She saved me today, but who knew what was in store the following day.

What I've failed to understand is why she went through so much trouble to get me back from my previous abusers. Once my wounds had healed from one experience, I was then "battered black and blue again".

There isn't much in life that I hate. I love my wife and children; that's a given. I love diversity, my profession, all sports, music, the arts, fashion, political debate, music, good wine, socializing with friends, eating out, golf, keeping fit.

I would say there wasn't much I disliked until I started this project. I won't go as far as calling it hatred; it was more like disgust. Do I have closure knowing he's no longer here, that he's dead in the ground? No. In a strange way, no. I don't have a clue why but for some strange reason, I still remember his birthday.

HELD AT GUNPOINT

During my years within the military, which is explained in more depth further on, I achieved a lot, did a lot, been there, done that a lot more. For the life and soul of me, I never would have imagined I would be held at gunpoint by friendlies, by my own.

It was obvious that recreational drugs where rife throughout the club scene. Anywhere there was a scene there were drugs, and the drug of choice for me and thousands of others was ecstasy.

The club scene in Germany was off the chart bonkers—techno, trance, queer house, techno house with some of the best European DJs spinning the finest tunes every weekend. So, what do you think a load of bored squaddies are going to do when they are off duty for the weekend? You guessed it. Get there rocks off; inexpensive, clean, and plentiful drugs; and go rave it up for forty-eight hours. We fucking loved it. It wasn't long before the brass across Germany suspected something wasn't all that it was supposed to be. They just didn't believe soldiers were getting truly and utterly smashed on fun drugs. "Lights out chap's, up early in the morning for more standing by your beds", I don't think so.

Beautiful, organised carnage every other weekend, coming back from raves thirty minutes before the start of my shift pinged off my eyeballs. It was easier when we were young. You just dug deep and cracked on with it with the least amount of eye contact possible. The youth of today go out, have a few beers, sniff a bit, and call sick for a week. Lightweights. Not that this is a competition.

In 1992, the biggest rave was hosted at the Olympic ice rink in

Koln, Germany. More than twenty thousand ravers were there to enjoy the hottest line-up of DJs. We rocked up mad for this rave, mad for it and it didn't disappoint. It was epic, the best rave hands down, twelve hours of bliss. Little did we know that across Germany, military police were getting ready for the biggest drugs arrest's in history.

We departed Koln in the late hours of the morning and headed back to camp. The five of us in the car were sniffing poppers and munching pills all the way home, buzzing. We drove into town, music blaring, we pulled up to the gates having half-heartedly tried to sort out our melons.

The gate swung open, a dozen military police, guns were cocked, and all aimed on us. *Fuck me. What the fuck is this shit?* I wondered, one MP shouted, "Hands up." Picture five smashed squaddies with their hands up in a car.

Another MP shouted, "Please step out of the fucking vehicle. Make your way to that wall and spread 'em." All the while we have loaded SLRs pointed at us. These cats were ready to do a job on us. It's not every day a soldier gets to fire off his weapon, let alone on guard duty in the barracks. 7.62m round travels 1450meters per second, it will kill an elephant a mile away. I guess we were fucking mincemeat if they'd have gone trigger happy.

What a head rush, we all stumbled to the wall, music still pumping threw our veins, legs stretched, arms in the air, ready to be searched. I know I had nothing on me, no weed, pills, or coke. I smoked and popped everything way before we reached camp.

We are searched while being screamed at. "You horrible little wankers! What the fuck are you supposed to be, 'gangsters'?" The car was searched, all the MPs found were a dozen bottles of poppers in the boot. "Right. Guard room, now!"

I had a good friend on guard room duty that day. As I walked past him, he whispered, "Refuse the piss test. Now this friend of mine was no ordinary friend. In 1989, I saved his life, yes, correct, it was I who prevented this soldier from departing the land of the living.

The stupid fucker was walking home pissed one night from the local nightclub, proper army pissed, there is no comparison how people get pissed today compared how soldiers drank way back then, there just isn't. He staggered past the only pub in town with a Turkish hit squad inside, enjoying their evening, singing Turkish songs about shagging donkeys as boys. He banged on the pub's window and shouted, "Come on, England! Come on, England!". If there is a bad move to be made in life this was is x10. Several armed-to-the-teeth death squad Turks swarmed out of the pub like hornets and went to town, I don't mean a slap on the cheek.

Long story short, to this day I don't have a clue how he managed to walk fifty-odd metres back to the barrack gates, get inside, and crawl to the guard room, where I was on duty that night. He had multiple stab wounds to his stomach, legs, and arms. This sapper was a pin cushion knocking on heaven's gate. His eyes were rolling back into their sockets, and there was hardly a pulse. There was no time for random chit-chat. I pulled several field bandages from the medical kit, along with two morphine jabs. In with the morphine and on with the bandages. In a nutshell, I was holding this fella's insides in the best I could. His intestines kept popping out from under the bandages. I was sure he was a goner; the blood loss was insane. I repeatedly shouted, "Stay with me!"

Several engineers joined me, working together trying to keep this soldier alive. He made it to the hospital alive, and miraculously survived the ordeal. So yes, he had my back that day.

In we go like convicts, heads down in shame. "Right, you, Auguste, first piss test."

As I walked into the room, I'm questioned regarding my whereabouts earlier that night. "I've been at my girlfriend's house, Sarge. These fellas just picked me up by the Commerce Bank. I flagged them down for a lift. I've got a shift in the officers' mess in fifteen minutes. I need to get showered and changed, Sarge. Oh, and for the record, I'm not taking any piss test. My missus will confirm I've been at hers all night." Okay, it was a bluff, but it worked.

"Well you better fuck off then and get ready for your shift." and that was that.

My commanding officer asked me a few days later if I attend the rave in Koln. I replied, "Not me, sir. That's not my thing. I fuck, fight, and cook, sir."

"That's my boy."

MARRIED TO COCAINE, PART 1: THE LOVE AFFAIR IS STRONG

In 2002 I finished a nine-month contract with Celebrity Cruises as a sous chef on a seven-day Alaskan cruise, cruising out of Vancouver, stopping off at Juneau, Ketchikan, Sitka, and the Hubbard glacier, which was very picturesque.

The entire food and beverage offering designed by the Roux brother, so being a sous chef onboard ship was a big deal. You were treated like an officer, you had privileges. I had to oversee all preparations and that dishes were served to specification during service. There were 3,200 passengers and 150 chefs. Food was available twenty hours per cruising day, so the output was insane. We worked seventeen-hour shifts seven days per week on a nine-month contract.

Once my contract ran its course, I flew from Vancouver into Heathrow to attend my brother's wedding. It was the wedding of son number 2 with Boris. Soon as I landed, I was on the gin and tonics on the train to Middle England. I arrived at Doris's residence wasted, put on my brave face, and went with the flow.

After a few hours' sleep, I picked up my partner at the time from the airport. We drove back into town, where I was fitted for my tuxedo, we shopped for a stunning outfit for my partner. Doris was divorced from Boris, so things at home were bearable apart from her excessive drinking, which she didn't hide, and her wicked tongue. The trick was not to get on the same level as it would only end in an argument, and you were exposed to the same slurs and verbal abuse I witnessed most days growing up.

Wedding, piss up, three courses, more booze, silly dancing, crap speeches, more silly dancing, fall over, Egyptian gymnastics, off to bed.

I had already secured a job for the coming winter, I was going to work as a freelance chef in the finest chalets in the French Alps. Snowboard all day, cook during the evening, DJ and consume drugs through the night. My partner and I had two months before the start of the season, so we decided to fly out to Italy and harvest grapes for a month. Best decision we ever made, though total bonkers. Up at 6 a.m., local breakfast, half a litre of wine, and then out to the vineyards.

Back at midday, another awesome local lunch—menu cooked by a demon old lady on the pans—more vino, and back out until early evening. Shower, change, another awesome meal, followed by stunning wine and a few spliffs. Winter season commences.

We drove to the Alps, set ourselves up in our tiny shared apartment, and on with the season, "twenty-four-hour party people". I was working at a very beautiful chalet for a wealthy executive for 70 euros per hour, plus tips and booze. One evening I was asked by a fella impressed by my culinary skills if I would like to fly to the Costa del Sol and look at a restaurant he and a partner were looking to procure. All expenses paid. Why not?

The following week I flew to Spain from Geneva. A hop skip and a jump, a short transfer, and I'm set up in a beautiful apartment overlooking the coast. That evening we ate the finest of meals, drank the best wine, and then off to the local disco, "skull fucked". Now this is where it gets surreal. The following morning, I'm stood in a massive, tropical-style restaurant with plastic palm trees, camels, and flamingos. The place resembled a plastic rainforest, very strange restaurant, run by Ze German's.

It was obvious the restaurant made a killing in the eighties, nineties, and early 2000s, but it was now suffering. The kitchen was a shithole. God knows how they did what they did, but obviously, they did what needed to be done. The location was bang on the beach. After an hour of over the head chit-chat in English Spanish,

German, and Geordie, I was asked what I would do if the restaurant were mine. I told them knock the fucking place to the ground and start again. After an awesome lunch, tapas with local wine, it was back to the mountains.

Before we knew it, I was back in Spain, looking at a shell. The restaurant had been procured, we built our dream restaurant. It had a huge terrace with an awesome bar. The kitchen was open, planned with a huge two-metre grill with all the mod cons, changing rooms, toilets and an office were at the rear.

My two partners were also friends with the financial backer, who hired a bar team from Spain. A week before opening, we all ended up at a beautiful nightclub close to the beach, a local club for the locals.

It was a very drug-free evening with loads of bubbles, banging tunes, and more Spanish snatch than locals at a bullfight. We staggered out of the club, hopped in a taxi, and went back to the villa. As soon as we were out of the resort, the cab driver turned to us and asked, "Coke, cocaine? You like da cocaine?

This dude had been scoping the new restaurant. He recognized us as new venture, new money, new prospects, new clients. Before he said, "aine", it was an instant yes. It was a small detour to the gypsy camp, this was no ordinary gypsy camp, it was huge. Caravans were everywhere, it was like the stage crew for Cirque de Soleil.

Everyone male, or anyone who looked like a male, was armed to the teeth; AK-47s machetes were everywhere. Fires were burning in oil drums, and meat was being barbecued. It was like Afghanistan, but the driver ensured our safety and said it wouldn't be like *Deliverance*.

The driver popped out and popped back in, we had cocaine, a lump the size of a Matchbox Car, solid, 90 per cent pure. "No cash. Pay tomorrow. I come restaurant." Fairfuckingdincum, we just invited Pablo to the party. Talk about living in the moment. I'd just spent a third of a million on a brand-new swanky restaurant and bar. What's there not to love about life? How does the saying go, "Live well so we can fucking die well"?

The opening party turned a few heads within the local community. Restauranteurs, local businesses, clubs, and our new friend Pablo the taxi driver were there. A wise man would have known getting in that taxi meant the restaurant was flat on its face before we opened. You give the keys of your Aston Martin to a Welsh boy racer from the valley and tell him not to go racing, what's he going to do? go racing.

Everything we had in Spain was at the expense of someone else. For me, it was the party, I was so naïve, I lacked so much in life. I was irresponsible, immature, and totally inappropriate at times, but something in the shadows was there, it had always been there.

Growing up without a care in the world, just pushing it to the limit every day, some might say that's rock and roll. But the amount of cocaine we consumed started to consume us. It consumed us all to the point we didn't know what the fuck we were doing. Morning, lunch, dinner, throughout service, days off, no fucking clue. Apart from that we had wasted a golden ticket opportunity.

I was long-boarding "skateboard" to work in just my board shorts, barefoot, coked to my eyeballs. Smoking it, snorting it, washing it, snorting the stuff off gas cookers, tits. I was spanking a grand a night in strip clubs. It was the "wolf of Wall Street" on the Costa Del Sol.

I started DJing in a local club around the corner from the restaurant. The owner of the club frequented our place a lot as we didn't close until the last customer left, and most evenings we were serving until the early hours. We started chatting one evening after a few glasses of vino that led to a few lines, "Yeah, I can DJ", blah, blah, blah. DJing, nightclubs, drugs, I had it all. Life was utterly bonkers. Life was triple bonkers.

I knew there was a problem when I started avoiding my business partners and workmates to stay home alone, sniffing coke and getting off my box on my own. I had everything at my fingertips to educate myself and gain experience, to grow up and become mature and responsible. But I just couldn't grasp the concept. No matter how hard I tried, something was missing. Something didn't connect. It was the live fast die young mentality.

The restaurant didn't last more than a year after opening, we snorted everything. One year of cannibalism, parties, clubs, coke, parties, clubs, coke, hookers. I, we had lost the plot.

KISSED BY GOD

August 2007, I set off from Ipswich down the A12, heading for London. I'd just been appointed the new executive head chef of one of the largest hotels in Europe. Nine hundred bedrooms, two conference centres, three kitchens, and a staff of 160 would who require breakfast, lunch, and dinner. Then I had the guests to feed a top of that.

I was responsible for the entire culinary department, 30 chefs, twelve kitchen porters, a multimillion-pound revenue stream, and all the whistles and stress that come with such a huge operation. I nailed the interview while I was working in Dubai as a head chef of the famous Après restaurant and pizzeria.

The restaurant Après overlooked the indoor ski slope located at the Mall of The Emirates. It was a beautiful shopping mall with the world's largest indoor ski slope, a bonus considering I was made for snowboarding. As a chef, I didn't mind split shifts at the restaurant as I could get a slide in before evening service.

A 120-seater all-day restaurant, I designed the menus, trained staff on the style of cuisine, implemented all health and safety policies, and managed the kitchen from the front to back. I spent three years in Dubai. I travelled well and lived the high life as well as any other expat. I made some awesome friends, survived two car crashes, sustained a broken collarbone on the indoor ski slope, partied with celebrities, and dated a few models.

As soon as Après opened, we had the media all over us. Justin Bishop, the general manager, who sadly passed away years later, was a fantastic PR man. He put Après on the Dubai dining scene. When it opened in 2006, the restaurant was runner-up for best brasserie in Dubai in the Time Out What's On awards.

Into the third year in the sandpit, I realized Dubai wasn't doing it for me. I just wasn't thinking straight. I started acting erratically. My mind was bouncing off walls; I just wasn't me. I was ripping into chefs. I couldn't concentrate during service let alone on life outside the kitchen. I was losing it, my mind was shot to pieces once again.

A CHEF LOSING THE PLOT

"You fucking, stupid, homosexual, dick-eating, kiddy-fiddling bastard, felching motherfucker." Swearing makes you nervous? Holy Mother of God. "Do you fuck your mother or eat your sister's pussy? I don't fucking believe it. You're a fucking chef, and you're telling me that when I swear in the fucking kitchen it makes you fucking nervous.

"Fuck off. Get out of my sight, you fucking prick. No, better still, eat shit and die 'because I'm going to fuck you up tonight, bitch bareback. You ever made love to a man?"

"No chef."

"Well tonight is your lucky night, baby. Me and you in the dry stores over the tinned tomatoes. Yeah, baby. Hey, fellas, who wants to join in and make it a spit roast? Mumbles, you fancy getting your load off tonight son."

"Absolutely, chef."

"Put some music on. Let's boogie."

"Hey, guys", said one of my devoted chefs.

Bruce don't fuck with me, I'll stab you in the eyeball Lee. That cock-eating sausage jockey has just told me I make him nervous when I swear in the kitchen."

Silence. Then hell breaks loose, there are sounds of laughter and chanting in several languages echoing out from the kitchen into the restaurant. I can't believe it chef. Lame-ass bastard. What a pussy dhal-eating prick."

Then the inevitable happened, rug-munching, bongo head, "been there done that, I've been in this industry years and I'm only twenty-three years old new girl"— "I'm a proper foodie", who called herself the restaurant manager—stuck her head in the kitchen, and like some ponced-up Nazi dinner lady, "What's going on? What's this commotion? Has someone been burnt, cut themselves?"

"No, I've just chopped matey girl's leg off."

"'Matey girl?' Who's matey girl?"

"Oh, and for the record, I'm about to deep fry Bruce Lee's head in the fryer, and when I'm done, how about you step into my office and rim me for a minute or two before service? I'd like that a lot."

A typical and immature way of responding to a manager, but that was me. Losing the plot was an understatement. Now I don't claim to be any kind of psychic but the look on her face told me two things: She was either going to make the first and biggest mistake in her new job and stamp her authority down. Or she was going to pretend to join in and have a giggle about something she has no idea or clue about.

Guns at the ready, backed by a small army of knife-wielding auks braced for battle and a young sous chef eager to make his mark on his chicklings, we were ready to go over the top.

Taking a deep breath, I braced myself. "What the hell is going on in here, chef? Tell your chefs to pipe down and carry on with their chores."

Like a lunatic on speed, I unleash what can only be described as madness to the outside world, normality in an everyday working kitchen. Or was it? No, I don't think it was. The next day the manager resigned.

2007 I realized I had a problem, a serious problem. That ticking time bomb from childhood had started to simmer nicely. I had moved to Dubai in 2005 wanting to start a fresh beginning, live a good and decent life, and make some good money.

My life-changing plan didn't work out, I packed up my life, headed back to the United Kingdom, and walked straight into a job that almost killed me, again. My first year I was trying to hold down a long-distance relationship. I travelled to Thailand and Australia, weekends away. We stayed in stunning hotels all over the world, but it just wasn't working. The relationship I was trying to hold down literally blinded me to the issues I needed to sort out in my head.

When the mind has decided to pull down the shutter,
we turn into clowns, we are beasts without purpose
or reason, we are nothing, we are not even human,
we are empty souls waiting for the bullet. **AK**

MARRIED TO COCAINE, PART 2: IT'S HOW IT ALL STARTED, MY LOVE FOR DRUGS.

I was introduced to the drugs menu when I joined the military. Some of you might have seen the movie *Buffalo Soldiers*. Staring Juaquin Phoenix, a bunch of degenerate American soldiers up to no good In Europe. Well what I and my army chums got up to trumps that movie, because that was a movie, what us marauders "degenerates" got up to, was the real version.

The UK rave scene was well and truly underway during the late eighties when I joined the military. My first rave would have been collision at the civic Hall in the West Midlands. Apart from a blast on some poppers and a few larger and blacks, I didn't touch drugs. For me, it was all about the music and the skirt.

I knew a lot of people were on ecstasy because of all the gurning going on; there was a big old gurning competition going on that night. I didn't have an addictive personality "yet". I'm still fucking surprised I had any sort of personality at all during those early years.

Moving to Germany from Middle England was like walking on the moon. I was in the military free to experience everything. Free from mother and marriage number 2. I was fed well and paid well, and it was time to grow up and become a man. Well I don't know about growing up like maturely growing up, or even becoming a man, well becoming a man but not a mature man, not a mature grown man in any shape or form.

LIFE IN THE MILITARY: RANKS AMONGST STARCH-PRESSED CHEFS

*P*TE—*Private (that's me), same as a commis chef.* A twat who gets bested and fucked with all day, day in and day out. "Go ask the chef for a long stand." "Fetch me a right-handed whisk." "Go fetch the legs of salmon and elbows of lamb from the chiller." "Chop that flour." "Peel those peas." "Suck my dick bitch, eat shit, and die."

No one wants to befriend you because you're seen as a liability, a custard-burning moron. Your only so-called friends are the German dish washers, who are mostly Holocaust survivors who don't speak a word of English other than phrases like, "Can you pass me that pan please?"

One chef, who became a good drinking mate over time, used to tease the shit out of me. "That's the only pussy you're going get in here, sunny Jim. Imagine eating her pussy out—that one, the one with the moustache and the wooden leg—after she's been scrubbing pots and pans for fourteen hours in the sweltering heat." And like a stupid, pumped-up yank, he would shout, "Get some, get some. Go on, son, get some." I never drank the dish pigs' tea either, something about the slice of bread and the pickled onion submerged at the bottom of the cup always baffled me. Must have had something to do with the war, maybe nouvelle pot-wash cuisine.

Then there was the civilian butcher known as Bandsaw five foot no inches Bill, who left the army and married a six-foot Bavarian goat herder called Dave, a fine woman, the kind of woman who would probably tear you a new arsehole if you stepped out of line. But Bandsaw Bill always seemed happy, he stayed in the same job in the same barracks in the same town as a civilian chef. Not sure if he and Dave had kids; never did see any one legged gremlins around camp.

Bandsaw Bill went through frozen carcasses like they were softened butter. Blade steak, rib chop, sirloin chop, centre lion ham slice, spare ribs, chuck, shank, brisket, round short plate, knee chop, best end neck cutlets, chump chops, middle neck, belly, and bacon. The place looked like a fucking dinosaur graveyard, Jurassic Park 12, mass slaughter Texas chainsaw massacre stuff seven days a week, day in and day out, long before I got there and probably long after.

When Bill left in the evening, the place was always pristine like a surgery, immaculate. This old soldier had never heard of HACCP or COSHH, just old-fashioned elbow grease and a damp cloth, "old school".

Johnny Bing Bong, the Pavarotti of the kitchen, always sang Hitler youth songs. By the way, he was Hitler youth, still with the blonde hair and blue eyes. He was a massive old dude, six-foot eight. His hands were like wheelbarrows. His pastries, puddings, and desserts were incredible, out of this world incredible.

He always used to make this one dessert, simple beyond belief. He took bread dough and rolled it out into a greased baking tray drenched with melted butter, sprinkled it with loads of granulated sugar and cinnamon powder baked it until golden. He turned it out, sliced it, and served with Chantilly cream, cream whipped with vanilla essence and icing sugar.

He also taught me every swear word in the German dictionary. *Sclamper, arsechluck,* and *pimmel kuff* were just a few of my favourites. Great if you're taunting the Nazi locals; bad if you're trying to pick up a six-foot hairy German girl with a Chris Waddle hairdo down at the local Star Wars bar, not good, not good for morale if you know what I mean, seven shades of shit proverbially kicked out of you.

Every now and then, to piss off Bill, Johnny Bing Bong would frog march up and down the workmen's entrance, yowling Nazi war songs at the top of his voice. It drove Bill up the fucking wall. After twenty minutes of Johnny's Eurovision song contest attempt, it was party time.

"Snap, bada boom, bada bing." The most passive chef I've ever known turned into a psychotic, raving, five-foot, axe-wielding lunatic, mumbling, "What about their legs? They don't need their legs. Umm, man flesh. Meat's back on the menu tonight, boys," like he was talking to a small army of Bandsaw enthusiasts.

More yowling. "Mein führer, it's mine, a yar, yar, yar. Right left, left right.

From the butchery, Bill responded, "You fucking sauerkraut-eating, Jew-killing motherfucker, baby slayer, I'll slice your fucking face off if you don't stop that cock-sucking Nazi bullshit." And that was just for starters.

Once the rest of the chefs got wind of what was going on, they all legged it to the back, like trailer trash rednecks, shouting, "Black dude outside. Let's roll." They then joined the ranks, like SS madmen, with Johnny Bing Bong at the helm, frog marching up and down, chanting and singing.

"The show is almost about to begin. Take your seats, ladies and gentlemen." Curtain rises, and bolts of lightning, out flew Bandsaw Bill from his cave, carving knives for lung chukers, Mr Miyagi's roundhouse spinning-bird kick, tigers' claw, drunken master, wax on, wax off. "What about their legs? They don't need their legs."

"What the fuck?"

Everyone scampered, ducking and diving for cover in imaginary trenches and bunkers. "Come on, you felching faggot fuckers. I'll turn every one of you into mother-fucking spare ribs if you think you can wind up Billy boy. Now piss off, ya bunch of twats." Knives slicing through the air, Bandsaw Bill gave the Ninja bow of respect and looked at me. My bottom lip was on the floor, catching pork scratchings. "Welcome to the barmy army son," and calmly returned to his colossal cutting machine.

No one got sliced up that day, but half of the chefs were in the medical centre with concussions, abrasions, and sprained wrists and ankles caused by diving through doorways and out of windows. The master of butchery a black belt in pork chops and is a living legend, Bandsaw Bill. As for Johnny, the master of chaos Bing Bong, you will always be my inspiration when it comes to the pastry section. Quite ironic when you think about it. Ex-Hitler youth inspiring a black lad from the Black Country. I suppose it was never meant to be.

Finally, the local German porn star salad server. She was not really a friend, more like an object of desire. She drove me crazy every pissing day because she was a triple fit German bird who wore her chef's trousers so tight you could see her piercing when she took her apron off. Plus, she was the only girl I've ever known to pull off an Austin Powers haircut, this girl was unique, way ahead of her time, it was her who started my fetish for any lady throwing a javelin in chefs whites, buff.

I'd daydream endlessly of her knocking the granny out of me, that was probably why I was always cutting my hands to smithereens. "Concentrate, chef," she would say in the most seductive male / female voice.

The lance jack, same as a CDP. A total bell end, the sort of person I would smash the fuck out of if I were on civvy street. Basically, a promoted chef who just spent three years acting like a fucking schoolboy, arse fucking the living shit out of the master chef and everyone below him. First stripe.

Corporal, same as a chef tournant. Same as a lance jack but with two stripes, and he's probably drilling the living daylights out of some German model who drives a Manta. Duties include playing football, squash, tennis, pool, and cards. They get their own bedroom and have a dependency for anything illegal and have a twisted fetish for porn movies which include glass tables and dangle berries.

Sergeant, like a sous chef. Now these fuckers don't act like sous chefs on civvy street, Oh, no. These bastards are as fucking ruthless, right horrible cunts; evil, conniving backstabbers; my misery. These fuckers made me scrub drain covers the size of Tesco's with a toothbrush.

They made me chip all the black secreted carbon off the bottoms of pots the size of bathtubs that have been in use since the war ended with a tooth pick. I had to scrub the bin area every fucking other day and drain scalding fat from the fryers. If I burnt myself, it was funny shit to those wankers. No first aiders back in those days, you got told, "fuck off to the medical centre".

I emptied stockpots the size of metal wheelie bins, the ones that sit at the bottom of skyscraper bin shoots. They also doubled as pasta boilers, soup cauldrons, and when the steamer broke, a potato boiler. Cleaning one of those bastards just after you've had a stock going for forty-eight hours was a cleaning hell.

Twenty minutes of back-breaking, soul-destroying hardship, and there were three of them, I would be ordered to scrub out brat pans with my fingernails until midnight. Plus, on top of that, trying to kick out half a dozen stoned chefs with the munchies before you closed was a fucking mission. Funny as fuck but a mission.

An extra. One solitary, painstaking extra can be scrubbing the entire kitchen floor with a toothbrush. I had seventy-five. Why? I suppose I was the only black chef in the entire brigade.

The master chef, same as an executive head chef. Hardcore as they come, old-timers, Lenny MacLean's in their day, total respect.

I'd just come off a shift in the officers' mess and back at my dormitory, which I shared with three other chefs. I showered and changed, a four-pack and snacks I was ready to enjoy my evening. But before I settled in two chefs walked into the dorm—no knock, just bowled in and locked the door behind them.

Here we go, my initiation in to the army catering corps, the first of many beatings. How wrong was I? I will call them the two Dave's, I believe they had been keeping an eye on me from the first day in the kitchen, checking me out. Out and about around town in clubs, bars, who I spoke with, and what I got up to. But it wasn't much to be honest, I was still finding my feet. "Do you fancy a smoke?"

"Cigarette, yeah sure."

"No, a smoke. Do you fancy a spliff with us?"

"Yeah, boy, this is the army. Yes or no?"

So, I was on the spot. The two Dave's were different. They dressed differently, designer clothes, they grew their hair as long as they possibly could, when off camp they wore earrings. They both dated German women, drove nice cars, and were handsome fellas, spit roast.

What isn't there to like about these chaps. Do I go with the flow or walk out of the dorm? "Fuck it, yeah, I'll have a smoke with you guys. But I must say I'm a virgin when it comes to this shit." They grinned at each other and began to build. Cherry popped, I was as stoned as a caveman in a cave.

I was in with the cool kids, proper cool kids, I started wearing designer clothes I pierced my ear. I went to different clubs and learnt how to party, speak the lingo. Before I knew it, we were driving to Amsterdam and other exotic places. I remember my first trip to the 'Dam like it was yesterday. I had just turned eighteen.

England, Germany, Amsterdam. Life was amazing; it was fucking awesome. So, when in Amsterdam, you do what people go to Amsterdam for, to get bang on it, and we got bang on it. You name a bar, I've been there. You name a club, I've done it, red-light district educated. Name any type of weed solid, I've smoked it.

Purple haze, Thai stick, skunk, orange bud, Sputnik, pollen, red or gold seal, pineapple, cheese, white widow. Then came the main course—cocaine, ecstasy, PCP, crack, speed, but I stayed away from smack. My alcohol consumption went out the window, as a matter of fact there was no window.

You might be wondering, *What next for the skinny shy boy from the black country, full-blown gangster?* No, not yet. I excelled at everything, everything my schoolteachers said I would be shit at. Football, athletics, I was all over it. I played football with a famous Scottish footballer, now the manager of a premier league team. We played on the best chefs' football team in Germany before he left the army and went professional.

I ran for my division, BAOR (British Army of the Rhine), competing all over Germany in the 100 metres (sub-11 sec.), 200 metres (sub-21), high jump 2 meters, I was also a member of the fastest 4 x 100 relay team in Germany at the time.

Now here's the thing, I fucking loved drugs; I was hooked. When

I was on leave I'd be at any number of clubs in the United Kingdom—Hummingbird, Quest, Wobble, Digbeth Institute. Over in Coventry, it would have been Eclipse, I was smashed out of my eyeballs, buzzing like a kipper wearing clobber you couldn't purchase in the United Kingdom at the time. Before the army I was wearing old man's, clothes robbed from a jumble sale.

I was making regular trips to Amsterdam with a few friends from the camp, stocking up on everything. You name it we had it—e's, weed, hash, coke. We had the lot, and everyone in camp wanted a slice of the cake. Twenty-four-hour-, forty-eight-hour drug lock-ins, organised raves at the local nightclub, going to work high as a kite, driving all over town on acid, it was total mayhem, mayhem years before anyone in the military got wind of what was going on.

Then the Gulf War happened. Greedy ass Saddam Hussain was sticking his nose into other people's oil stocks, it was the flip of a coin which sent me to war, I was off to join the allied forces and take back Kuwait.

Hey private, here's a joke for you, "how do you stop five niggers raping a woman? Throw them a basketball", fucking twat.

CHEF'S EQUIPMENT FOR WAR

There is nothing in the desert and no man needs nothing

SLR—self-loading rifle, 7.26-millimetre rounds, 1450 meters per second; four-ton Bedford truck with enough rations to last six months; rocket launcher, dustbin cook set; number 4 cook set, twelve by twelve cooks' tent; four sets of nuclear biological chemical warfare (NBC) suits; 4 nerve gas epee pens; 55-millimetre Browning attached to the cockpit of the Bedford, a very big machine gun.

Before deployment, all soldiers, regardless of trade, had the chemical warfare menu. It wasn't a choice menu; you had all dishes, including the standard anthrax injection and the nerve agent pre-treatment (NAPS set). This war was different. Saddam Hussain was a lunatic, and he wasn't scared to use chemical weapons.

The number 4 cook set looked like a metal suitcase when closed. A little bit like a picnic table, you lowered the legs and then open out the table. There were four burners and a small metal oven which came separately. You just sat it on top of the burners; it was useless for baking. It came with two temperatures, hot or fucking hot, so anything that went in had to be watched with a keen eye.

The cook set ran on petrol, I filled the tank which was part of the contraption and pumped air into the system with a bicycle pump which would pressurize and then pass the gas through another pipe and out through the burners. So, you literally were cooking on gas.

Though a remarkable piece of equipment, it was a bastard to maintain and a fucker to clean. Rumours had it one blew up and robbed a chef of an arm. Mine leaked petrol all the time. I just filled the bottom with sand to soak it up. Fuck knows what would have happened if it went up. I would most likely be walking round today minus one arm and half my face.

The dust bin was an actual dust bin, but you placed a metal piece shaped like a doughnut with a tube up the side and then a chimney on the bottom. On the side of the bin you attached a petrol tank with a tap which would drip droplets of petrol into the bottom of the doughnut. Once the petrol hit the bottom, it would ignite "explosion" and heat the inside of the doughnut. When the bin was full of water and tins of food, it would come to a boil within fifteen minutes.

Army rations combined with a little imagination weren't half bad. Each box had a different menu. inside

A—Baby's heads, otherwise known to a squaddie as steak and kidney pudding. It apparently resembled a baby's head when pushed out of the tin. This came with mixed-fruit pudding (MFP), vegetables, dried potato powder, and oatmeal biscuits (which were magic for making porridge). You had to soak the bastards overnight as they were hard as nails. Forget about dunking them in your tea, one biscuit would soak up the entire cup.

B—Chicken curry, my favourite, although it didn't come with endless amounts of poppadum, mango chutney, lime pickles, and naan bread, this recipe came with rice, tinned fruit salad and a few other bits one being a can opener, no quick release pull like you have today.

C—Stewing steak which was great for making pies if you had a few fresh rations, which we did every second week—eggs, flour, pasta, herbs and spices, fresh fruit, and meat. Also, in the ration boxes came tinned luncheon meat, beans, donkey meat sausages, powdered milk, tea, coffee, and sugar.

D—I have totally forgotten what was in that cardboard box, but there were biscuits hard bastard.

From what I can remember, the first few weeks where spent driving around the desert with my squadron, testing out our gear. I was obviously along for the ride to keep them fed and watered.

Sitting here twenty-nine years later, trying to write this chapter, trying to remember what life was like for those six months as a nineteen-year-old desert rat chef in the thick of it 24/7, believe me I had to put a few bottles of vino away to complete this chapter.

I'm not going to write about death and destruction, it was inevitable and something I'd rather not share with you, but I will later anyways. I haven't a clue how I got to this point must have been the pills. Sitting on the end of my number 4 cook set one afternoon before the ground attack, which lasted only a few weeks, with the end my rifle stuck in my mouth, my finger on the trigger, safety off, one in the chamber, shaking and crying, ready to end it all was the beginning of the end, the first time I contemplated suicide, and it wasn't because of war. I just had the perfect opportunity to do it.

THE FRYING PAN

There are a few stories which stand out from the chaos of war. One of them involves a frying pan, a fucking frying pan. We had just set up camp. It was early afternoon, and I was stretching my legs around the harbour area when I came up on a battered old frying pan, in the middle of the desert. This wasn't a frying you could rub and boom, Will Smith appears, oh no, I might have been in an Arabian desert, but this was war.

This thing was fucked, It looked like it had been run over by an entire army. The handle was hanging off, and the sides were bent back. But when I rubbed the sand from the inside, it had a non-stick base, something rare in army-issue pots and pans.

I took the pan back to my field "desert" kitchen and gave it a good seeing to. I smashed the sides back as best I could with a spanner. Then I screwed the handle back and taped it with duct tape. Gave the fella a good wash and proved it with salt on my petrol burner. Then I gave it a good wipe with grease.

A few days prior we had picked up fresh rations of flour, eggs, fruit, and vegetables. So, after reincarnating my frying pan, the only thing I could think of which was fitting for supper was Spanish omelettes, a dish I hadn't made since college and one the lads would not be expecting that night. Most likely a wholesome all-in-one stew with powdered mash and MFP for dessert.

I prepared all the veggies and taking in to consideration I had to knock the omelettes out quickly, I precooked the vegetables. I cracked, whisked, and seasoned the eggs with pepper and got ready for service for forty lads using one non-stick pan. I also prepared jacket potatoes and beans.

It was around seven. The sun was setting, and boy what a sight is was, a huge red ball of fire disappearing beyond the sand dunes. One of the sergeants strolled over to my cooks' tent to see how I was faring. "Evening, Private."

"Evening, Sarge."

"What's on the menu tonight then?"

"Spanish omelettes, jacket spuds, and beans."

"Bollocks," replied the sarge.

"Honestly, Sarge, no fucking around." I opened the flaps "easy", to my tent and there to his surprise was my mise en place, ready for service.

Within ten minutes, all the boys had turned up and formed an orderly queue outside, ready for a feed. "What's for tea, sloppo?" Sloppo is another term for army chef, who served slop to his men.

"Spanish omelettes, ya cunt."

"Yeah, get fucked."

I strolled behind my number 4, cranked up the heat, popped on my apron, uncovered my mise en place, and started the show. "Omelette, eh?"

"Yes please, sloppo," he answered with a startled look. He turned and shouted down the queue, "Chef's really cooking fucking omelettes."

Three or four omelettes in, the pan was well seasoned and in full swing. The first two had stuck a little, but I wasn't going to give in. Ten omelettes down the line, and I was on fire. The burners were pumping out maximum pressure, and the oven was acting as a plate warmer for the spuds, the beans were bubbling away nicely. Temperature inside my cooks' tent, 140+.

"You're a madman," shouted one squaddie. "This omelette is fucking to die for." It would have been quite ironic if a Scud missile had fallen short of Bagdad and blown us all to kingdom come.

"You're welcome. Enjoy." The sergeants stood back and watched

91

as I cooked, tossed, and served piping hot tasty omelettes to my fellow desert rats.

The sweat was pouring off me. My tent didn't have the luxury of extraction or AC, just a cool breeze wafting through my tent. After twenty minutes, I had fed all the lads, including the top brass.

I was so pumped and buzzed out I wasn't hungry. I just skulled a bottle of water. That night I didn't wash a thing or prep a morsel for breakfast the following morning. The old boys knew they had seen something never seen before during active service.

I received a standing ovation and a pat on the back. One of the sergeants came over and asked where I purchased the frying pan. "I found it, Sarge, over there."

"You're a legend. The boys are well impressed with their omelettes. They were expecting the usual."

"Not this time, Sarge. A few eggs, a chef, and his pan, and it's all gravy, baby."

"Less of the baby, Private. I'm old enough to be your dad."

"Yes, Sarge."

I don't know what happened to that pan, I just seem to have lost it. Anyways I hope it's with a Saudi or Kuwaiti nomad, being used for what it was created for, cooking on gas.

NEAR-DEATH EXPERIENCE

After the carpet bombing, we were well on our way to Kuwait A1 Escalon, just behind the main battle group. There was no hanging around. Most of our movement was at night, full power ahead, there was no time for error or school boy mistakes, this was war, you fuck up, people die, your friends die, you die.

Sleep deprivation and being in an NBC suit twenty-four hours a day was tough to say the least. My driver taught me how to drive the Bedford, hour on, hour off. This was hardcore trucking cannonball run with missiles, fighter jets, apache helicopters overhead.

We stopped for an hour, so it was un-pack the dust bin, spark it up, and feed the lads. It must have been midnight. The bin was full of tins bubbling away, A, B, C and D all mixed together a super stew for supper.

I set up a table with tea and coffee, milk and biscuits. I must have been two to three metres from the Bedford. "Fire regulations, hmm."

I stared to open the tins to empty the contents into serving containers when the Sarge came running over. "Sloppo, you fucking lunatic. We need to move this shit to the back of the truck now and quick fucking sharpish."

Chop fucking chop. I could sense the Sarge was in a panic. Three others came to help, and it was all hands on, moving my little canteen set. "What's going on, Sarge? What's the panic?"

"Just move, boy."

We dragged the bin full of tins and boiling water and the tables to the back of the truck. What happened next brought me to my knees.

In the distance I heard a rumbling sound, the earth beneath my feet stared to shake. All around me sand was being whisked up by the howling wind. The air was hot, and it was difficult to breathe. The rumbling noise got closer.

It was impossible to see more than thirty metres ahead of you in the darkness. Then headlights came out of nowhere. Moving at full speed, a whole squadron of Chieftain tanks sped past right where I had my little canteen ready to serve supper to the lads.

I was on my knees, watching in amazement, gobsmacked. If the Sarge had come over five minutes later, I would have been brown bread dead, splatted all over the desert and that would have been the end of that, no more pages to read.

IF IT HAD BEEN NERVE GAS,
I WOULD BE DEAD

Being on the move every day and night was really taking its toll. You don't really understand true willpower and determination until you're involved in a real-life war situation. Having to unpack and repack two or three times a day, off load and on load all your cooking equipment fuel, weapons, and rations in the wind, rain, pitch-black after driving hundreds of miles through the desert with multi-launch rocket systems (MLRS) flying over your head was truly a test of stamina.

One evening we had just moved into our harbour area. The boys had dug in, and I was still setting up my cook's tent. The wind was howling, and it was pissing down.

Trying to do this singlehandedly was mind-bending exhausting. After an hour or so, I had my tent up, but I was piss wet threw, shattered, and starving. But there was no time for rest. I had to get food on for the lads.

Outside of every harbour area a chemical weapons alarm system was set up. It sounds a high-pitch siren as soon as it detects any form of chemical weapon. The siren was so loud it would most likely wake up a piss head in the gutter in Bangkok on a stag do.

Tins in the bin, I'm good to set up my sleeping quarters, two dozen boxes of rations with a dos bag on top. Five-star luxury considering the circumstance. Out of fucking nowhere I hear a high-pitch siren.

WTF? This isn't the time to finish off a mid-wank while your eyes are watering with joy.

Military procedure states you have nine seconds to get your gas mask on, a fine piece of kit compared to what the Yanks had at the time. Nine fucking seconds. It's nine seconds whether you live or perish. Many of you might have watched *The Rock*, an epic movie in which bad guys rob a chemical warfare depot, move into Alcatraz, bad guy drops the nerve gas, his skin bubbles, eyes pop out, tongue turns into a three-piece sofa, his balls turn into popcorn then he dies a slow and horrible death.

Well I didn't get my gas mask on in nine seconds due to exhaustion and several other factors, one of them being I had my dick in my hand. Overcome with some sort of outer-body experience, my brain fooled me into thinking I'd just received an uppercut of nerve agent.

Gas mask finally on, I'm crippled. I have another handful of seconds to get into full NBC kit; it's not happening, epee pen smashed into the top of my thigh. I give into fate and except the fact that I'm about to rock up at the Pearly Gates or hell with two wraps of cocaine, a few crushed ecstasy pills, two acid tabs, skunkweed and forty-eight boxes of army rations and 20 B&H.

When I came to, I'm propped up against several boxes of rations with an epee pen hanging out of my thigh and my gas mask off. The Sarge was standing over me. "Private, are you okay, son? Son, do you hear me? If you hear me, nod your head. If you can hear me, nod." My head rocks back and forth, he takes it as a yes and demands that food be ready in 30.

PRISONER OF WAR

The purpose of the carpet bombing the 1st stage of the allied forces attack was to annihilate the main highway to Basra and everything in Iraq that resembled a military stronghold. The main command from Schwarzkopf was if anything moved, destroy it. This was the first time I had seen death and destruction on a scale that still has an overwhelming impact on me to this day. We had to cross the highway to Basra on our way to Kuwait, where we would be stationed just outside the city a few days before Saddam Hussain admitted defeat and surrendered.

I said I wouldn't talk about death and destruction earlier but the stench, nothing compared to it. The place itself cannot be compared to any blockbuster movie. I have seen the sun set in places which only tells me heaven is here on earth. I have snowboarded in mountains with crystal-blue skies which only tells me heaven is here on earth. I have seen beauty in the eyes of my wife and children. I have cooked stocks and sauces which have stopped me in my tracks. I have cooked and tasted food which can only be compared to great sex. Heaven is here on earth so is hell.

What we witnessed, me and my fellow men, those few days was something else. The sky was scorched black with smoke from burning oil wells. Cars, trucks, lorries were still smouldering, and the stench of burnt flesh and hair made your eyes water. Snap, crackle, and pop from fires still burning. Camels splattered all over what was once the highway. Bomb craters the size of Olympic swimming pools. When you have truly witnessed what another man can do to another man, your outlook on life becomes very different. What gets me to this day, almost thirty years after the first Gulf War, is the smell, the burning rotten smell of flesh.

We set up camp a few miles from the highway, my tent was up, my kitchen was set, and my bed was made. So, I decided to take a stroll around with my driver, helmets, body armour, SLR, and our wits.

We must have been gone ten minutes when out of the blue, out from a trench came one solitary man who had been hiding for God knows how long. Soon as he noticed us, his hands went up in the air, he shouted the only words he probably knew in the English language, "Surrender."

No messing around rifles with the safety off and a bullet in the barrel, aiming straight at the enemy, or was he the enemy, this guy was fucked. Was I going to kill a man today, could I kill a man if I had to? Yes, I would have put one in his head without even thinking about it if he had flinched or made any random gestures. Looking at that moment from the flipside today, if I had blown that guy's head off, or did I? Am I making this next part up, if I hadn't, would my life have been better, because it hasn't been any better, I've always been tormented. As he got closer, I could see he was wearing pink flip-flops—pink flip-flops, "bonkers" utilities and an army jacket two sizes too small.

"On your fucking knees. Get on your fucking knees, hands behind your head. Now." I might have forgotten to mention in the army you're a soldier before anything. That's what they teach you in basic training.

We bound his hands and took him back to the harbour area. We informed our sarge, who came over to my tent, "Fucking conscripts, Harmless bastards. Feed him, water him, and then he's off to one of the POW camps."

I dressed down and then sparked up my burner. I got a tin of stewing steak and beans. I gave the POW a bowl of water, soap, and a towel, and kept a close eye on him, I couldn't keep my eyes off him, it was weird, what was he doing wearing pink fucking flip-flops. The way he washed it seemed liked he hadn't washed for months. He was so meticulous. I'd never witnessed anyone appreciate something so basic.

When he finished, I gave him a set of combats and socks, sat him down, and gave him the hot bowl of stew and beans I had prepared. If I only knew then what I know now, a piece of Arabic bread would have been a treat. He ate all the beans and left the stew. "No like meat only beans, boss" so the fucker does English, cheeky cunt.

"Sorry it's not halal, mate." Fussy bastard.

When we departed, he began to cry. I could see the fear in his eyes, I told him everything would be okay. What could he be so scared of? I was to find out years later, after leaving the army, when the war was over, and the prisoners of war were released, most conscripts where shot dead in the desert on mass for surrendering.

The power, the force, and strength of the ground attack would have been too much even for a well-equipped military force. But thousands of conscripts were dragged from their homes to fight. Not a chance in hell my man, not a chance in hell against the biggest ground offensive of vehicles moving at one time since D-day, fact.

I have many other memories of the war, like the time I almost chopped off my hand and sprayed blood all over the kitchen on R & R, getting stoned in the dunes, fighting, drinking my own brew made from tinned fruit salad on Christmas Day.

Watching Scud missiles launched, flying over our heads during the night on their way to take out a tactical command centre, or a village or town. The Gulf War taught me many things as a human being, to appreciate life and all the trimmings, it taught me discipline, or so I thought. PTSD had hidden itself in the deepest parts of my brain, waiting silent, ready to pounce,

My co-driver perished two decades later, blown to smithereens by an IED in Iraq. Love and peace to you my brother, may your soul travel well for eternity.

When I returned to Germany, I received a commendation by the commanding chief of the allied forces for outstanding services during the Gulf Conflict. Many soldiers receive this award for bravery, aptitude, professionalism, and upholding military values. I believe I received mine for those omelettes.

My reputation with the brass was squeaky clean because I represented the regiment and won medals for athletics, football, cross country and the odd biathlon. I departed the army in 1992, when my three-year contract with the military had run its course. My military conduct was exemplary.

2007

It was my first Christmas party at the hotel in which the woman I would marry twelve years later was also in attendance. One of the most amazing chefs I've had the pleasure of working with was also in attendance.

My journey with this chef will be kept private, sadly, he was taken from this world way too early, leaving a beautiful partner and children behind. May you find eternal peace with the angels my brother. There isn't a day goes by that you are not in my thoughts.

It's not going to be easy telling you this fractured part of my journey. It would require me to write another book, so, we'll dive right in. Cocaine is like Pringles, once you've popped, that's it, you're on the Pringle train.

By the way my issues with my mental health are still simmering on the back burner. To be honest, I've totally given up on that subject because now I'm in fifth gear, managing this beast of a kitchen.

2008, I move into a lovely two-bedroom flat and need to sort out a local deal as I'm new to the area, the quiver I've been getting isn't cutting it anymore, nose garbage. Who's the man who knows a man? Anyone looking for a nose in any London hotel knows it's the concierge team. A few phone calls and a text message, I'm hooked up.

I'm in, and this was where and when the whole fucking party went south, and I don't mean south like I've popped to the coast for the weekend or flown to Cape Town for bultong. If south was a planet it wouldn't be in our solar system. Work five days, get bang on it all weekend, back to work Monday morning feeling wavy. Work five days, get bang on all weekend, back to work wavy. Repeat. It becomes routine, and that's the killer—routine, work, cocaine, alcohol, work, repeat, repeat, repeat.

Before I know, it's the norm. This is who I am, a functioning fantastic junkie. I was still procuring my gear from the same dealer when one evening he said, "Listen, fella, you've been getting the £45 .7 nose buffet. Try this. It's the £60 .5 Bolivian."

"Why not? I'll take three." By the way, I'm earning good money. I have no kids which means I'm snorting thousands of pounds every month.

My routine took a turn, I started knocking off early on Fridays, just after lunch. I'd meet my guy; bang boom cocaine sorted; Friday Saturday Sunday bang on it. Wavy Monday. Tuesday I'm feeling ok-ish.

2008 is over, nothing has been sorted regarding my simmering stock of plutonium, carrots, onions and bouquet garni. My simmering pan begins to mutate into other forms of mental health and illnesses. Did I have a clue? No, I did not. PTSD became CPTSD, scarier version of the latter.

With cocaine comes an avalanche of other goodies, including extreme alcohol abuse, extreme addiction to porn, and sleeping with a multitude of casual fuck buddies with the huge risk of contracting all sorts of nasties. Believe me, when you're out there, and I mean orbiting some planet no one has ever heard of, the last thing on your mind is protection.

I was holding down the job but now taking risks, Mondays were a no go, and Fridays were a blur. I was having major comedowns on Mondays after a crazy weekend. I'd be sick as a pig on Tuesdays and have wavy Wednesdays. I would be back on top on Thursdays only to think about scoring my gear on Fridays.

I forgot to mention unless I was out on a Friday or Saturday night, which was rare, I'd be home doing all this coke alone. I seldom did it with anyone else, until I meet a crazy Maltese fella. Cocaine was my mistress, I'd I had become a full-blown junkie, that's a lie I've always been a junkie. Calling the ambulance was a regular thing, A&E was a regular thing, I was that guy you walk past in the street and say, "what a loser". But guess what? as far as I was concerned, I was fine. I was in tip-top shape, on top of the world, enjoying life.

The years started to pass me by, weight was falling off me like conkers from a tree, I was snorting half a gram per line. I'd hold up paranoid in my flat, curtains closed, with my boxers on at two in the afternoon. I would be covered in cream and feathers. Paranoid as fuck I kept looking through the letter box thinking I was going to be busted by a huge furry bunny rabbit smacked off his bunny ears.

Finally, hope, my future wife moved in, but I was living in denial, cocaine was still the lady running things in the yard. I had lost all sense of decency, all sense of identity. I cannot relate to love, I cannot relate to reason, I can't even relate to reality. I had overdosed several times. I was six foot three and weighed sixty-five kilograms. I was a dead man walking. I'm still ashamed of that person, that version of me and the things I did to my wife.

There are things I did that I can't discuss, but any junkie alcoholic will know the depths we slump to. Some junkies come back; some are still out there, waiting for death to come to them. I had lost the will to live. I had lost the will to be part of anything, without my wife being there, adíos to me, adíos in the ground.

Why did I want to die so much? was suicide the only way out, out of what, what was it that I couldn't grasp? What was I ignoring? Had the pot simmering on the back burner well and truly exploded? In 2013, I walked into my GP's office, broke down and begged for help.

The years between 2013 and 2020 have been the hardest journey I've ever taken, a journey back to life. A journey which literally killed me. I had to stare death in the face, and only when I knew the meaning of life, the *true* meaning of life and all its wonder, death would finally move on and seek out another victim.

January 2020, I assumed I was doing well, I was physically and mentally stable, but out of the blue with no warning came death and he came at his most powerful. His cloak wrapped tight suffocating me. I could feel my soul departing my carcase, soon to be splattered all over the motorway.

If the truth be told, I had slipped in and out of a few jobs, big jobs across the country, and the journey back to life was taking its toll. I had been in and out, and through the NHS system numerous times, prescribed all kinds of drugs, had more assessments than I can remember, and referred to various clinics across the county.

My OCD irrational thoughts were getting stronger. I was having frequent anxiety attacks. I was super-hypervigilant every day. My nightmares were off the charts, I thought I was ok, what a twat. On top of all that, I started to hallucinate without the acid. I hallucinated while walking down the street, in bed, in the shower. I was tripping without the LSD, or was it those tabs we munched back in the days, I don't think so?

While all this was going on, to add fuel to the fire, I decided to apply for Master Chef Professionals 2020, and that's was when everything intensified tenfold. My mental health went haywire. After two very successful telephone interviews with MCP, I decided to start practicing my signature dish. I'm sure you are familiar with MCP and the competition format. In brief, there is a skills test, followed by a signature dish, the knockout stage, an invention test, and another knockout stage. Then you cook for the critics, it's life changing.

I was invited for the audition stage in Camden, London. I was very confident and positive regarding the audition. I was geared up and in what I thought was a good headspace. All my senses and thought processes were super-intensified.

I was also in talks with a friend and in the process of setting up a pop-up food stall, Biriyani Bobs. Work was busy, and my food was getting mad crazy positive feedback. We were taking more private functions and bookings for weddings, birthday parties, and bar mitzvahs than ever before, and moreover, I was hosting a monthly chef's table.

On top of all that, I was at the gym every other evening, taking a testosterone booster, BCA, creatine, and drinking protein shakes. On 6 January 2020, I left work. I had already practiced my signature dish a dozen times in my head that day, but I needed to finalize the garnish.

By the time I pulled on to the M25 at jt19, my thoughts were travelling at lightning speed, I had no control of my thought process whatsoever. My thinking became dark, I was wrapped in a cold, grey blanket, and I could hear my thoughts speaking to me as clear as day. My breathing was erratic; I was hyperventilating. I felt a weight on my chest I could not shift, it was him, I knew it was him, he had finally come for me.

I told myself, *End it now. Just pull the car over and end it. Pull over and walk into traffic.* I could hear these thoughts in my head as clear as day. *It will be quick, painless, I promise you. Just pull over and walk into rush-hour traffic.* To say I was scared was an understatement. I was past scared. I was trapped within a cloaking force around me. I was possessed and needed more than a priest. The end of my days had finally come. But was this how I would go out, suicide, I'd toyed with the idea for decades, so why not.

This was the day I was going to leave behind two amazing children and a loving wife. I turned on my indicator light to pull onto the hard shoulder. Full beam headlights in my rear shone like an exploding star and the volume from the horn was like a nuclear explosion, the earth shock beneath me, my senses were on the outside of my body, lights flashing all around me, the temperature in the car was 20 below zero. Think of it as you wish, I believe that a greater force was at play that evening, call it what will, a greater power maybe, my guardian angel, I do not know. What I do know there is reason why I've written this book.

Decades of denial, ignorance, stupidity, drug and alcohol addiction, CPTSD, anxiety, years of being super hypervigilant. Years of carnage and damage I had done to others in my head, mainly loved ones. The destruction I caused upon myself finally caught up with me driving home from work, driving home from work of all things.

I arrived home in an absolute pickle, erratic vision, my head traveling at light speed. I look at the knife in the kitchen sink, contemplating if I should drive it through my heart. My wife knew something was seriously wrong. Quivering uncontrollably, I blurted out my mental health. Straightaway she was on the phone to the crisis team. Within minutes I was speaking with a crisis team member. I was on the phone for what seemed eternity before I came back down to earth, bruised, battered, somewhat lifeless, mentally broken, my mind in a million pieces like a smashed vase and a donkey was trying to put it back together.

At nine the following morning, I had my first assessment with a crisis team psychologist and psychiatric nurse. This was going to be first time my wife would hear the true extent of the abuse inflicted on me as a child and the horrors I experienced during my deployment as a desert rat during the first Gulf War.

This was the beginning of the end. This was the start of enhanced trauma pathway treatment and cognitive behavioural therapy (CBT) for adults suffering with extreme CPTSD. The non-existent relationship with my biological parents, with whom I tried so hard to reconnect, finally burnt out. It never felt natural to me anyway. Every phone call or facetime was an effort, I felt they were clinging to me for their own self-pity or for some sort of closure to the past.

It wasn't me who needed them. They needed me, those few minutes with me every other week over the phone, so that they might feel in some sort of weird, twisted, toxic way that I might have forgiven them both. 2nd quarter 2020, after lengthy consideration, I decided I had to let them go. For me to get my head straight and live life without distraction, I needed to do this. I finally plucked up the courage to walk away and turn my back on my biological parents, my terms my decision.

JUST ANOTHER COCAINE SESSION

An ounce of coke works out to be twenty-two or twenty-four wraps, depending on how much you are prepared to cut it. I went halves with a fellow chef, half for him half for me. Not sure what his plans were; I didn't really give a fuck, sell half, make his money, get high and try and fuck some bitches, I really didn't care I had a half ounce of block, not crumble or repress. Half ounce of crystal all to myself.

I left work pumped on a Thursday afternoon and drove straight to the off-licence. I picked up two litres Jack Daniels, a bottle of vodka, a large bottle of lemonade, forty Marlborough lights and cheesy snacks and headed straight to my apartment. My flatmate had gone to Germany, so I had the place all to myself.

Down to my boxers, I started snorting Thursday afternoon and stopped Monday afternoon. The flat was totally and utterly wrecked, fear and loathing. There was blood on most of the towels in my en-suite bathroom. Blood on the carpets on both sides of my bed on the walls, cigarette butts everywhere. A murky haze filled the entire apartment which resembled a Mexican smack den.

I'd suffered considerable blood loss, I was covered in moisturising cream, I was unable to speak and struggling to breathe. I was a dead man walking, death seemed to have walked straight through me. Death had been with me those four days. Death had always been with me. Did I care, no, so I chopped out the last fat line and collapsed.

Dancing with death, knocking on its door for so many years, willing him to let me in, I realised my efforts were futile. A bullet to the head would have sufficed. I had the one chance during the first Gulf War.

After those four days locked in my apartment, I came out of there different. Fucked yes, but something had clicked. The one thing I learnt was if I couldn't die, I'd better start living, hence my recovery. My guardian angel isn't in hell; nor is she in heaven. I believe, I truly believe to this day I hadn't even meet her yet, or knew who she was, or were she was traveling form.

SWEETS

One summer's evening back in the early eighties, I remember Boris and Doris calling us in from the yard, "hey kids who wants some sweets", sweets, fuck yeah. We only got sweets at Christmas or when we robbed money from the church. Like ravaged wolves we stood there shaking with joy. If I give treats to my children today I hand them to them. The bastard of a man threw the sweets to the floor, we went for them like dogs, like savages. I looked up to him, he was laughing, look at those animals.

THE RUSTY BIKE

That's what they called it, the rusty bike in the shed. I was never going to be anything to him other than his wife's mistake. It was all about his two sons, and baby three, a daughter, had arrived.

You would most likely think that all kids in the same household would be treated equally, but as you already know, not this kid. I was treated with so much disregard I would have had no issue with being left with my auntie in Ipswich until old enough to fend for myself at eighteen.

Our estate was weirdly odd, a weirdly odd council estate. I can't put my finger on it to be honest. We lived on the main road running through the estate. You had Flowery Gardens, where the KKK, Phillis and Teddy, lived. Thinking about it now, wherever we moved, they would move. When we moved across town, they followed.

Most family gatherings just ended in fights. Too much booze with way too many emotions, all of us witnessing the most horrific of fights amongst adults. For us kids at Christmas we were guaranteed WWE. Once Christmas dinner was consumed, there would be a good old scrap between Phillis, Teddy, Boris, Doris, and anyone else brave enough to spend the day with what can only be described as the most dysfunctional family on the estate.

I and half the estate witnessed my mother kick shit out of our neighbour years after this rusty bike incident; it was a proper grange hill scrap. As a kid I suffered with asthma. On a scale of 1 to 10, I'd say it was a 9, during the summer months, 10. Straight to the point. I'm out kicking bricks around with other kids in the large car park at the back of our house. I felt my chest tighten, it tightened so much it felt like a heart attack, or how I imagined a heart attack would feel, or as if someone had jumped on me and sat on my chest.

I managed to walk inside and using a sort of sign language, indicated to her that I was having an asthma attack. I was really struggling to breathe. There was no inhaler to be found anywhere. By the way, this isn't me slapping lipstick on a pig. This was how it happened. I'm now in a serious condition, wheezing heavily, every morsel of air keeping me in the fight.

What does she do? She doesn't rush me to A&E, like any other mother would do, or call an ambulance knowing full well they would have treatment for such an attack. She led me upstairs, put me on my bunk, and left me there. She fucking left me. My son falls over outside, and I'm all over him. Falls of a ride in the park, I'm there. On holiday, he doesn't leave our sides. Hawk eyes with tender loving care. That's me, and it was the same with our beautiful daughter.

To all parents, what would you do if your child was having a full-blown asthma attack and you didn't have an inhaler? Looking back in anger and disgust at the neglect, all the verbal, mental, and physical abuse, it dawned on me the perfect opportunity to use an asthma attack as an unfortunate death. I must have passed out as I do not remember anything after being taken upstairs.

Why else would you leave a child a child having a force 10 asthma attack? It's blatantly obvious they didn't want me, and I will leave this world knowing that.

The last half term before the summer holidays, most families across the United Kingdom are planning holidays. A cheeky week away before summer. I was out back with the rest of the runts, kicking bricks again about the car park. "Get in here, now." It doesn't take a giraffe to figure out this had all been planned out beforehand.

Boris and Doris have decided they are all going on holiday. Well, everyone except me. Now I wasn't old enough to look after myself, and I knew I wasn't going to Ipswich, let alone stay with the gestapo who lived on the same estate. No.

So, if I wasn't going to stay with any member of our immediate family, who the fuck was I going to stay with for a week? "Me and your dad are taking the kids on holiday," Doris said. He wasn't my fucking dad. I didn't have a dad, I had a ware wolf.

I didn't think there was anything possibly left for her to shame me with, but then came the triple-decker, shit, pubic-hair sandwich. "You're staying with Claire." Claire was our next-door neighbour's "grange hill scrap". I was ten at the time. I remember because that year I started senior school.

"But why Claire, Mom?"

"I'm not having this conversation now. You're staying with Claire, and that's that." That's right, staying with Claire for the week, speechless, mind-boggling speechless.

This was how low they were. She lied through her teeth. She convinced me that it would be worth my while. She and Boris agreed that when they returned, I would get a brand-new racer, a new road bike to cycle to school on.

Jesus Christ! A brand-new bike from the bike shop in town. Now any kid who had walked past that shop in town knew the bikes in there were top of the pops. I was stoked, proper stoked, over the moon. Okay deal. I'd stay with Claire.

They all fucked off to wherever it was they were going. The plane didn't crash because they all came home a week later. All nice and tanned, all looking like leather suitcases and all wearing fake Lacoste. Socks, T-shirts, shorts, wristbands and headbands, Lacoste lock fucking stock. Turkey! I knew it. I knew they were fake because all the crocodiles came off in the wash.

Why did I really think I was going to get a new bike? Because I was a child, and I thought this was real, a new bike. Wrong. They had no intention of buying me a new bike. I got the rusty dust bucket in the shed. Shame, shame on me. The piss royal taken out of me by everyone and all who saw me riding that piece of shit.

The laughing stock of the family, the estate and the laughing stock of school. That year both my halflings received brand-new bikes from that shop in town. While I've been writing this, I purchased a beautiful Conondale road bike. Cost a few pennies, but it's the first road bike I've bought for myself. No reason just wanted to buy a new bike.

IT REALLY DID HAPPEN

Ever sat in a stadium packed to the rafters and contemplated the fact that you're the only one there? Or sat in your own living room, wife nagging you to death, kids clinging to the ceiling and felt like you're not even in the room? Well maybe not because of the, "wife nagging you to death," but just felt you were somewhere else, in another dimension, another world, a place you haven't been able to figure out.

Haven't been able to figure out where or what or when or even how it's possible to sit in your own living room and be a million miles away, in another dimension, "Babe, babe, babe. Hello, anyone there? Knock, knock."

"Oh, sorry babe. What was that? Did you want something?", I've suffered with being distant for years.

I was asked by my physiologist how life was at home, how my relationship was with my wife and kids. Yeah, fine. We get by. Blah, blah, blah. But then it dawned on me. Physically I'm there, but mentally, I'm off somewhere else. I'm off somewhere else, trying to solve the universe's greatest mysteries. Nope, I'm trying to figure out what I've just missed in the last five minutes and contemplating why I've done the weeks shopping in Aldi wearing a G-string in high heels with a huge pink afro?

Until you place content into a blank space or thought of some trigger, you'll be out there in cuckoo land for a long time. My trigger was my sister. I needed something to trigger a process, a "Yes it did fucking happen"-type trigger. Or a "No, it didn't happen" trigger.

I spent years looking past things, through things, over things. I was seldom in the moment, never there physically, mentally or emotionally. I suppose that's another reason why I did so many stupid things, because I never thought it was real.

The period in question were the months, years before I could remember, remember the feeling of a shitty nappy, warm milk, being rocked to sleep or winded, being thrown in the air only for the person to step aside and watch me bounce off the pavement. Or how I became covered in bite marks and bruises as a baby. It's obvious I would have felt that pain, but I can't remember. Me being distant was me trying to take myself back there. That's all it was. No great scientific reasoning. I just wanted and needed to know.

I had to hear it; I had to be told it. There isn't a parent out there who is going to admit to his or her middle-age son that as a baby, he was thrown across a room or had his lunch poured over his head because he couldn't communicate like an adult.

My sister told me the state I was in as a baby. It wasn't good; it wasn't good at all. I'm not able to trust anyone, any family member today because of lies. The people I believe committed such abuse are no longer with us or hiding behind evil masks. Why would anyone own up to such horrors, most likely to protect the dead or keep the guilty hidden?

My biological parents will continue to hide themselves behind whatever it is they know, but they will not confess to anything out of shame. Over the years, they've had every opportunity to speak with me as I have been the bigger man and put myself in front of them on numerous occasions. Even when I was at my lowest, I had some sort of will to want to know why me, why me? and still no answers. I'm over trying anymore, hence why I've turned the page and moved on. My goldfish attention span wasn't because I was being an asshole or an arrogant up my own arse thing. I was just trying my hardest to understand what I didn't know, know about me.

ICE CUBES AND JACK

Another stinking year. Our firstborn was two, and I was in the darkest of dark places. My relationship was non-existent. Looking back, I hadn't a clue how my wife was coping with me until a few years later, when I started sweeping up the debris.

My wife was pulling her hair out because of the damage I was causing, so I decided it was time for me to move out. I packed my entire life into the boot of my car and headed to Ipswich, the one place I found peace.

I had been forced to resign from my current position, a constructive dismissal. I was paid three months gardening leave, so I had plenty of cheddar to see me through until I found something part time. I had also started legal proceedings which was also going to consume me as well as the hard drugs and liquor I was devouring.

The one decent thing which came out of this was my wife agreed at the time I could take our firstborn every other weekend. I'd drive south, pick up our daughter, and drive back Ipswich. I'd spend two amazing days with her and then drive her back Sunday evening or Monday morning. The only two day in the month I was half sober.

On the drive back, and every drive back, I stopped off to pick up an eighth of coke from a reputable dealer and a four-pack of special brew from the shop next door. By the time I had driven back to my temporary home I was wasted.

I had lost my job and was suing the hotel. I was slowly losing my daughter. I'd lost the will to function, and now I was dealing drugs. The inside of my nose was flesh raw. There was blood on every bank note I had in my wallet, and when I couldn't snort, I would smoke cocaine until my nose had healed enough to vacuum some more, which was approximately an hour or two.

My diet was also shot to pieces. A chef having worked in three Michelin-star kitchens and managed some of the busiest kitchens and largest hotels in the United Kingdom, I was nowhere near five a day. When I did eat it was ice cubes in a large Jack Daniels. I'd wake up in the most random places, wrecked and hugging a bottle of Jack with a note sticking out of my nose.

The meeting that should have never happened in my current state. I'd arranged a meeting with my biological father on the outskirts of town at a swanky restaurant frequented by football players, top brass, and bigwigs from the city. My objective was to ask questions, listen, observe, and mentally document. If answers slotted into those blank spaces, objectives were achieved.

I arrived at the restaurant first. I ordered a large Jack and lemonade and sorted the table. BF rocks up, smart, clean-cut. We were escorted to our tables and given menus and nibbles. We got a bottle of plummy red, and the chit-chat got underway. "So how did you meet my mother?" I thought the answer would have been more tasteful and somewhat respectful, considering I was looking for some sort of closure.

The dog shit that poured from his mouth was done in the most disrespectful and condescending way. A first-class cunt with no consideration for anybody apart from himself. "Son, I first saw your mom working at the same factory I was working at. Jesus, she had legs from her neck to the floor, a beautiful rack, and a backside to die for. Son, I said to myself, 'I've got to have a slice of that woman.'" By the way, he said this in a deep, believe it or not, seductive accent.

Second bottle, main course done, and he was still going on about his greatest conquest. I was gobsmacked. I just sat there, along for the ride. It was pathetic. Now regarding my current state, this fella didn't care the slightest bit.

Those objectives that I had sorted were futile. This man who sat in front of me had been doing what he had done to my mother to dozens of women. Now I didn't feel sorry for Doris. I really didn't.

I decided enough was enough. I'd had my fill of Mr Self-Righteous, and I had to get out of his face. We went halves on the bill, hugged, and we went our separate ways. On the way back to town, I called a dealer, scored a quarter of sniff, and headed to my mate's place to get on it.

I was strapped in, ready for the wave to break over me. I had no intention of seeing the sunrise. We sniffed, we drank, we sniffed more and more and more, we drank, and then I drove home to my air bed. I arrived home in six pieces, sniffed, had more to drink, and then decided dihydrocodeine and tramadol would be my cheese course half a dozen of each swilled down with Jack, Lights out.

A few hours later I make my way down stairs to the kitchen to pour myself a nice glass of chilled water. Feeling fresh and pallet quenched I make my way back upstairs, I open the door to my bedroom. As I slip into bed I feel the presence of someone else, I turn to look, it's me looking at myself sleeping.

I felt the slightest pat on my check, my eyes slowly opened. My cousin was sitting on the floor next to my blow-up mattress. She knew I went to see BF yesterday, and she was the only one who knew were my head was. "You need to come back to us. Please come back to us," she said. "They don't deserve you. Just let them go. Just let them fucking go."

Those words she whispered stayed with me, stayed with until I did what needed to be done.

A week later I interviewed for a vacant executive chef post for a celebrity. My résumé popped up on social media, and they were keen to meet me. I knew the set-up as I had taken my daughter there a few times when she was with me for the weekend. It was a busy place, popular with many residents from across the county.

The first interview was with the HR department. The interview went very well, so I went out and got smashed. I just couldn't help myself. The second interview, with the owner's wife, also went well, also so I went out and got smashed again. Third and final interview was midweek with the man himself at the farm.

The night before I had a few cheeky lines with a matey in town knowing full well I had to be in shape the following morning. Couple hours sleep, up, showered, dressed, and off for my interview. Fuck knows how I pulled off the interview, but I answered all questions and made some good recommendations to capture more revenue.

He was proper keen and invited me back for a cook-off. Seriously, I mean fuck. Third interview nailed, and they want me back for a cook-off to be executive chef for a shitty 25k.

We shook hands, he told me I'd hear from HR to schedule the cook-off. It was 10 a.m. I pulled out of the car park, pissed off, and headed into town for a liquid breakfast and to get bang on it. The place I found so much peace as a kid growing up in the seventies, eighties, and the best part of the nineties, I was going to die here, die a fucking junkie. A lot of people would have most likely said, "I fucking told you so."

During my 8th or 9th pint and into my 2nd ticket I noticed a missed call, so I listened to my voicemail. "Hi, this is Smile Hospitality. Would you be interested in a relief executive chef position in Shropshire. They are willing to pay £30ph until a suitable candidate is appointed. If you're interested, please give me a call at your earliest convenience."

The following morning, I had a short conversation with Smile Hospitality. I accepted the relief position and travelled up that Sunday to start Monday. The road back home had just begun, but first I had to sort out this kitchen. And it did need sorting out; it was a shithole.

The kitchen brigade was strong but lacked morale and a chef at the helm. Within weeks I had bought front and back of house together, departmental harmony. I had sacked several chefs, well told them to go fish. I had engaged with the sales team and regained the hotels 5-star health & safety food hygiene rating, plus bought all financials into line. These quick results gave the GM and the operational manager confidence in me and the team.

Its wasn't long before I was introduced to the hotel dealer, it wasn't Bolivian, but it would do, it got my rocks off and that's all I needed to escape into my own world. A chef with no filter propped up at the bar in my chefs' whites on ordering bottles of Don Perignon, thinking he's the man on top of the world, wrong.

Now that management had backed off I started to consume more olives and pickles, why, because they had just let a junkie into there house. Battling with addiction I didn't need an excuse, a pat on the back for doing well. Good day, bad bay, hard day in the office it didn't matter I was an addict.

The thing was, I wasn't the only member of the executive team bang on it. Anyone who has worked in the hospitality industry, either is or knows someone who is bang on it, using the quiver to get through there day.

I mean how else is the average human who isn't doing a 9 to 5, on their feet for 16+ hours without proper breaks is getting through their day? shredded wheat and red bull? I don't think so. The industry is in turmoil, If you keep your mouth shut and crack on with your day, achieve your KPI's, attend management meetings clean shaven, make the GM and the business shit loads of profit its game on to sniff that shit all day every day.

THE HAZINESS OF REALITY

The first time I met my biological father is the first-time thing which stands out the most. It was my birthday. I didn't have a clue what was going on behind the scenes; I was totally oblivious to what my auntie was cooking up.

The day prior I was out with friends. We had been out all day, drinking, getting high, and then we hit the clubs around town. Push Your Luck at the Caribbean club was on the menu that night. It was a shame what happened to that venue a decade later. The council knocked it down and turned it into a car park, a fucking car park.

Throughout the nineties, after-parties where the big thing. We got smashed at Push Your Luck and once kicked out, went on to half a dozen parties across town. I would be up for two or three days with ease.

Saturday night turned into Sunday morning. Most Sundays I visited my auntie, take my washing round, get cleaned up and have lunch with her; it was a social visit. She knew full well I liked the party life. I used to get juiced up on acid and speed when I was visiting while on leave during my army years before hitting the town. I smuggled back different types of weed and got everyone in the household stoned immaculate, proper, nice, warm, fuzzy stoned.

I left the after-party late morning, taxi to mine, picked up a change of clothes and my bag of washing, then took a short stroll to Christchurch Street. The day was amazing, sunny skies and a warm breeze. It was beautiful. I was still buzzing from the night and had been buzzing all morning.

I arrived at my auntie's house and was greeted with a warm hug and a kiss on the cheek. She knew I was flying, but I was never on the smack, so we were cool. Lunch smelled nice, roast chicken with all the trimmings. Umm, might not get much down apart from liquid in the form of alcohol. Cold beers were calling me.

My auntie treated me like her own son, and I treated her with the upmost respect, like a mother until she passed away of cancer in 2004. One cannot describe the loss to our family. We were truly heart broken.

I popped upstairs to the bathroom, before I jumped in the shower, I popped half an ecstasy tablet "green apples". I was just topping myself up, getting ready for an afternoon on the beers at the pub with my party people. Feeling fresh with a nice little buzz going on, I made my way downstairs. I told Auntie I was flying and asked if she could skip the main course and go straight to the dessert.

Apple crumble with custard. I passed on the crumble and swallowed the soft stuff. *Ding dong,* the doorbell rang. My auntie was all jittery and excited. "I've got a surprise for you. A surprise." Hey, a surprise. I rubbed my hands together. A surprise. Happy days! The gang had come over for a Sunday afternoon mash up. Nope.

My auntie answered the door. "Hi, come on in. He's through there." She walked this fella straight into the breakfast room, where I sat, having my dessert. "Hello, son, I'm your father." That was the first fucking time I heard such a phrase. "Hello, son." It echoed throughout the entire house, through my flesh, my bones. I was utterly and astronomically shocked. Where the fuck had this come from? I was buzzing and there was another buzz in the post, my senses had just been triple fucked, utterly triple fucked.

We hugged, more him than me; mine was more of an air hug, like hugging a total stranger. Well he was a stranger, I didn't know this fella. I was now in a state of shock and buzzing. He was talking, but nothing was registering. I'd lost the power to speak.

Battered, buzzing like a kipper, I said, "Let's go to the pub," and head for the door. Black Father Christmas and my auntie were hot on my heels. I set off quick, sharpish, and made a beeline for the pub, thinking about that first fizzy frosted glass of beer or maybe a nice fresh stick of wriggles and me not forgetting I was being chased by zombies.

The pub was packed. All my party people were cramped into the small beer garden. Pills and wraps were being passed under the wooden tables, friends were in and out of the toilets every five minutes. There was a buzz around the garden, it was electric, sun shining on every beautiful face. There were groups chit-chatting and smiley friends chewing their faces off.

I was handed a beer and a pill. I threw the pill to the back of my throat and knocked it down with a slurp. It was a beautiful day, but I was not feeling the vibe. Black father Christmas and auntie Stella arrive and join me at my table.

I was trying to keep it together when Johnny bent over towards me and whispered in my ear, "How's it going? How's it going? Really, how's it fucking going?" How the fuck is what going. He then said, "Stay off the drugs, son." That was the first piece of advice given to me by Johnny, as opposed to, "Would you like a bedtime story, milk and cookies before bedtime, a back rub maybe?" No, it was, "Stay off the drugs." I was on the fucking drugs because I loved them. It allowed me to escape, escape reality. I was doing drugs because there was something very fucking wrong with what's going on inside my head. It was he who was wrong, turning up that day was a bad move.

One of my friends asked me who I was with, and in slow motion, I replied, "This is my popohnny."

She replied, "That's nice. He's come to visit you on your birthday." I told her this was the first time I'd met him.

The beer garden fell silent. Half my friends' jaws dropped to the floor, as shocked as I was. "What a head fuck. What a fucking head fuck. So, you're telling me this is the first time you've met your dad?"

Yes, that first for me that afternoon was also a first for many of my friends. Apologies if that afternoon messed your heads up as much as it did mine.

My thoughts were racing. There was no control of what I was thinking. Thousands of kids may never meet their real parents, but when they do, they will most likely be better prepared than I was. I didn't know if I was coming up, coming down, or going sideways. I was coming up on another pill ready to blow my brains to marshmallow island. I whispered to a few friends, "I'm going to take a walk, get my head together." I excused myself from the table, kissed my auntie Stella on the cheek, shook Johnny's hand, and floated away.

I headed to the local park. I walked to the biggest tree and sat underneath it. I sat there until the early evening, staring into space and trying to piece together what the fuck had just happened. I never spoke with my auntie about that day. We never sat down and discussed the experience, how I felt, if I felt anything now that I had come face-to-face with my biological father.

I didn't feel anything. It was a blur, the haziness of reality, that period in my life, I found it difficult to feel anything, let alone love, especially the love for a man who had just walked into my life. I wasn't prepared. Nor was he. But he could have been, he could have really gotten his shit together and tried. After all, he knew way in advance he was meeting me. But at the end of the day, I was just one in a dozen of kids he spawned, so why the fuck would he come prepared.

WASTE OF TIME

When you've repeatedly been told by everyone you'll amount to nothing, put down, and be verbally and emotionally abused, something clicks upstairs. For me it was proving to everyone who beat down on me that I was going to do it, that I was going to have the final say, be somebody, but at what cost?

What was it going to cost me, really cost me? In January 2020, I was with my psychologist at the crisis centre. It had been about two weeks since my psychotic breakdown, and I was barely stable. The question, another million-dollar question was, "Why?" Why the fuck an obsession had become an addiction, and besides the drugs and alcohol, this was one addiction that was truly in my shadow all along. It was with me all the way, from the day I started my 1st work experience.

My kids and I were walking through Windsor on a sunny day. We were making funny shapes with our bodies and laughing out loud at our shadows. It was harmless fun until you think about your shadow and what may be looking back at you, what you can't see or touch or have control over is the spooky feeling within.

As I obsessed more about proving my family wrong, I lost all sense of why I was doing the things I was doing and everything I had done. I moulded myself so tight not to be like any of them that the identity, my purpose for searching, wasn't even within reaching distance.

I started living when faced with two end of line options. One, you end it here today, or two, you let it all go. Let what all go? Sounds simple, right? Wrong. When you've been addicted to something, something I didn't have a clue what it was, I realised at the precise moment everything I was trying to prove wasn't for me, nothing had ever been for me.

I wasted decades trying to prove to a family that didn't care if I was dead or alive that I was going to make something of myself. Sucker, that's me, wrapped so tightly I had been walking through my life blinded by the abuse I knew was always there until I had the balls to ask questions and speak out.

I suppose that's why everyone has fallen silent. They've all crawled back into their miserable, pathetic lives knowing I know. I fucking know. I stood so proud at my pass-out parade without you there. I stood so proud at every chef's competition. I stood proud when our children were born, at our wedding. Why? Because I did in fact achieve something, and I've got everything to live for, everything.

You may have wired my brain like a fruit kebab, but my dance with you all is done. Everything I do from this day forward I do for me, for my family, *my* family, my wife and children. You had your chance, I can no longer be shamed.

I've fallen and risen more times than I can remember. I've battered my body senseless, black and blue. I have danced with the devil, driven myself to the edges of darkness, and there's still one thing I cannot deal with today, no matter how hard I try.

Praise. When we praise people our kids, wife, family, friends, anyone—we release the feel-good vibe, a huge surge of dopamine followed by a smile from ear to ear. It gives our kids focus, motivation to do better, to achieve more, to want more of that feel-good vibe. But there is a flipside to praise.

If you're constantly putting your kids down, telling them they are useless, a waste of space, constantly criticising them, their brains have an adverse reaction. In other words, they experience downers. Persistent criticism breeds resentment and defiance, and totally undermines a child's initiative, confidence, and sense of purpose in the world.

Without a purpose in the world, I felt worthless. My only way to deal with this was to become obsessed with proving my family wrong. And where did that get me? Nowhere. Not being able to deal with praise has also caused issues in my life. I would respond to a compliment such as, "Nice chicken dish, chef,". There is no surge of dopamine, no smile from ear to ear. I just crack on with what I must do. And then came the criticism from others. "Did you see chef, how he dealt with that compliment? He's so arrogant, thinking he's better than anyone else." How far from the fucking truth? It's not that I'm arrogant, I just shy away from praise.

Or there's the subservient smile, a smile with no emotion, a smile to keep everyone happy, an obeying smile. I had a full-blown argument with my wife years ago. I was writing out Christmas cards and she said, "Babe, you've got such nice handwriting." She stood there and kept watching me write these cards. I felt so uncomfortable I told her to piss off.

COCAINE IN A NUTSHELL

First line 1988, last line 2019. Was it the ultimate love affair, the ultimate high? Hell no, fuck no. Would I do it again? I honestly do not have the answer to that question. The question I will ask myself is, Did I get away with murder? Absolutely.

Cocaine in a nutshell is nasty. It's up there with smack. As a middle-aged man today, when I do go out with friends—and it's not often—it was an excuse for everyone to get bang on it. WhatsApp messages back and forth weeks before the big night. "Have you called the dealer? I've got my tickle sorted." We'd all meet at a fancy restaurant. Half the boys wouldn't order as they would already be grinding their teeth putting beers away like a kid with a bag skittles.

Nightclub, I don't think so. It off to some skanky strip club, sat there for two hours talking bollocks to some fit bird from eastern Europe with a fake rack snorting ping off the corner of your credit card, asking the same question repeatedly, "Can I touch you? Please, just a little. Maybe a finger."

Still talking bollocks with a jaw at nine o'clock. It's a bottle of bubbles because she has persuaded you to spunk 250 large, "free bubbles". You get kicked out at closing time. You're knee deep in shit because you're broke as a bandit, and there are bills that still need to be paid. You arrive home just to jerk off to babe station, nursing a come down that lasts a week.

Would I get back on the biscuit train, would I do another hit? Fuck no, it's taken me the best part a decade to get off it, so I suppose that answers my question.

SUCKER FOR PUNISHMENT

Shortly after I moved back to the UK from Dubai and having legally changed my name for personal reasons, one being the fact I had the same surname as Doris's first marriage which didn't sit well with me. I had to rid myself of history and become my own man. I stupidly persuaded myself to contact Johnny, to see if he was interested in meeting with me. A good catch up was needed and for me to see what the man was all about, where he lived, what his life was like and to gain more understanding who my biological father was, and what he had achieved in life. This single not well thought out decision would drive me deeper into addiction, it was in fact the trigger.

It's a shame I didn't have such a wonderful phycologist like I do today back then, she might have said, "I don't think it's a good idea you take such a huge leap of faith considering you delicate situation", well shit happens, and the meet was set.

I decided to drive up north to meet Johnny, plus several of his children would be in attendance. To be honest I had no idea what I was getting myself into. It wasn't the smartest move, but like most other stupid irrational moves I've made in the past this seemed rational.

I set off early Friday morning with the intention of spending a long weekend up north with a family I never knew existed until a few weeks back. Thirty minutes out it's too late, I'm in the zone, off the motor way heading straight into the unforeseen storm. Why have I decided at this chaotic period in my life to be in his presence. It's simple, I want to be accepted, I wanted to know I was loved, I want to be told, that although they were irresponsible parents they both wanted the best for me, the best start in life so to speak. ""

The estate was a shamble's, it looked and felt wrong, apocalyptic, wrong like a war had just ended. I had a bad feeling about the next five minutes let alone felt good about spending the entire weekend here. If the shit hits the fan, well then, the shits hits the fan.

I've landed, passport at the ready for immigration control, this place doesn't look like England. I pull into what appears to be a car park, slash five aside football wasteland type pitch. I exit the car and head towards the beer jungle.

I was greeted by a dozen members of the family and their friends and the kids of their friends. Punched in the brown, kicked in the ribs, beaten black & blue, I hadn't even sipped a beer, my brain couldn't figure out what my eyes were seeing. Half a dozen clones, and their clones had little baby clones. A family of cloned half breeds, I need a line of chop to get my head straight. I'm tripping without the acid, hell comes to frog town and planet of the apes mashed into one. A foreign country surrounded by scary cloned people. This man's seed was atomic strong, even friends of the family looked like they had a splash of the man's genes.

From the off I sense something is south of the border, me, not only from down south up north. Finally, after decades, several of my half siblings have finally meet the man the child who without a doubt, one or two might blame for the mess they had to live through as kids, when Johnny decided to pick rhubarb from another mans garden.

The beers start to flow as I'm slowly introduced to the Harlem globetrotters, one by one. Being a wise man, and a connoisseur of the white stuff, it's obvious there's more devil's dandruff being consumed then there is beer in this drinking house. A patron has just exited the watering closet, it appears they have just stuck their head into a barrel of sherbet dip.

The conversation is intense, Peter and Simon a few years younger than me were cold. They were not interested in chit chat, small talk, getting to know me as such. They were in and out of the toilet playing some form of nose tag. Not happy bunnies, or the gear they were sniffing was nose garbage, not in my pocket, I've got the ping, the Bolivian flake. I'm not up for being responsible in giving anyone a heart attack today, so I keep my wrap for my nose.

Day drifted into night, it's warming up to be a proper cluster fuck of a gathering, there's a sense that someone has a lot of explaining to do. Four marriages, four sets of siblings and an army of kids and a bastard thrown into the mix. The mood changes dramatically, out of now where, Peter starts kicking off, in my face, "I don't give a fuck who you are Cus, no one here does, you're just a cunt, spawned from a one-night fling".

Tell me something I don't know already, I'm here because black Hugh Hefner needs to explain shit. Back in my face, "He fucked our mom over bruv, just like he did to yours". "Beat her, beat us, he's not a nice person cus, don't get to close for your own good". I take his words of anger and frustration on the chin, I haven't walked in his shoes, so I can't assume what I'm being told is, or isn't true.

The only half siblings that don't come across as cold are his two eldest girls, real nice, laid back and respectful to what is going on. After a few hours my head is an emotional mess, a sucker for punishment, I should not be here, my bad. I've nailed to many beers, I'm now on the JD's and lemonade, plus I've had two cheeky ones up the hooter of the corner of my bankcard, just to keep me in the fight, to see me through this nightmare on elm street.

There're tears, laughter, it's a crazy ride of emotions, but it's not long before the night takes a turn for the worst. Peter and Simon are juiced and buzzing their chops off, the other half sibling Marcus hasn't said a word to me all day. He comes across as a smug little wanker, there is nothing at all which I can relate too, all bar atomic seamen which connects me to this individual. He looks at me with disgust, like I shouldn't be here, he may have been bang on the money, I shouldn't be here, I don't belong here.

It's starting to sink in, that I'm in a world of no man's land, it's too late to drive 5hrs back to the shire off my nut, so I crack on and go with the flow as best as humanly possible. In a nutshell I'm in the wrong town, the wrong country and its Friday night in frog town. Piss heads, dust heads everywhere, and one fella with a foreign accent. The mood of the pub isn't a nice one, tension, beat up aggression, a pipe bomb ready to explode. The savage of all savages who's been eye balling me for the past hour with a strange head twitch from behind the bar, comes over to me, bends down and whispers in my ear "can you score some Niki Lauder me old fruit".

Gobsmacked with what I've just been asked, there is now another fella in my ear, who has appeared from nowhere, out the fucking blue, like a black genie. "You my brother from another mother, he wanted you here, so he could parade you in front of us all as his love child. Imagine that, all us lot being told you're his love child, while all he did was screw our mothers over. You don't mean anything to him, and I bet neither did your mother, how do you feel about that brother".

I leave the chaos of the pub, and sit outside nursing my Jack Daniels, why was I here, what was I looking for. I wasn't looking or searching for this detritus, tears run down my cheek, head in my hands shaking. I decide to call it a night and drive to Johnny's house, ripped, buzzing, pissed, peeled as a banana, without no consideration I was over the limit, there was no limit, just a broken, busted up addict, with no purpose.

I wait outside Johnny's place for an hour, Johnny arrives by taxi, come on son let's get inside and have a chat. Trust me, I'm in no mood for small talk, I'm beat, I'm off to bed. It must have been 3am, I'm woken by a loud thud, Peter and Marcus are kicking off in the living room with Johnny.

It's not nice what I'm hearing, it's not nice at all, these two cats have got issues and want questions answered, so do I, I have a ton of questions, but I guess it's not the time for my kangaroo hearing. Their voices fade, I drift off into a drunken sweaty sleep. I'm up early hung over in a strange place totally disorientated, not good for moral. I freshen up, black Hugh Hefner is in the kitchen, the only words from my mouth, I've seen and heard enough and leave.

I WAS THINKING ABOUT YOU

A year before, Doris explained to me that she abandoned me. We were sitting one evening in the garden, a beautiful evening. I asked if she had any form of security for later life, a plan B so to speak.

She explained she hadn't thought about yesterday, let alone what her future had to hold. I cut to the chase and explained she could purchase the house she had occupied for decades from the council if she wanted.

"Oh, that sounds too complicated," Doris said. After some convert station and convincing, we acquired the relevant paperwork and proceeded with the process. No one else had considered the welfare of their mother, let alone considered that a council house, a five-bedroom townhouse over three floors with reception, a garden the size of a five-a-side football pitch and driveway for three cars was worth anything. They all mocked the place.

Several months later, we purchased the property, market value was a nice surprise. She finally had peace of mind, they could go about their retirement knowing that they could relax and enjoy life. The house that brought so much misery throughout years she finally owned. She finally had security, something I seldom experienced as a child.

THE BEGINNING

I must confess it was my amazing daughter who brought me back. She gave me purpose in this world, dead or alive, buried six feet under, looking at all the miracles happening above my grave, brain dead, in an institution in a straitjacket, bouncing off four walls. Really.

There was only one way to go when my beautiful girl was born. Even before you came into our world, decades before I met Mommy, long before I was born. Millions of years ago, you started your journey across an ocean of stars and the eternity of space to help me through my darkest days.

I've truly danced with the devil. I wandered helplessly through the graveyard of my soul. I pondered for decades about my purpose. You were my guardian angel; it was you who gave me hope, it was you who showed me how to love, it was you who guided me towards the light.

My beautiful boy, without you this project would probably still be sat in the depths of my mind. Watching you grow has literally stopped me in my tracks, my little superhero, little do you know, but the light that shines from you and your sister has given me true purpose in this world, I belong to you and you are mine, always and forever.

My darling wife, I'm humbled by your forgiveness, I'm bonded to you for eternity.

My auntie Stella, I know it was you I saw in Ibiza and I know it was you who pocked me in the ribs at the funeral. You may have passed away many moons ago, but I know it was you I saw. I walked across the swimming pool area to make my way to the beach. No one else around, no one. You turned around to look at me and waved from your sun lounger. The halo around you was breath-taking, and the smile on your face sent electricity through me. I know you are in a good place. You were happy. You looked so happy knowing your two beautiful children and I are okay.

This project was started many years ago, miraculously, I've achieved the unachievable, don't ever let anyone tell you, that you can't achieve great things. To all those suffering with mental health issues or survivors of childhood abuse. living with trauma, or those who have sadly taken their own lives, the forgotten souls, I dedicate this book to you all. May our voices be heard.

Auguste Knuckles x

THE JOURNEY HASN'T ENDED

After departing the Army, I moved to one of the craziest and most beautiful cities in the UK, crazy in a good way, in every way. The rave scene for me had ran its course, it got a little to moody. I was looking for something new, something different and I found it in Bristol.

The scene was off the charts, a beautiful mash up of intelligent drum & bass and seductive soulful, funky house. My church would become the legendary club Lakota. Addicted to Bristol's night life and everything the city had to throw at me, my love for house music was born, it was engraved deep inside.

I spent years tearing up dance floors, I had to try and do everything once, a human tornado oblivious to time, life was good. All I needed was my small circle of close friends, house music and drugs, lots of drugs. I guess that psychedelic, apocalyptic part of my life will be told in another book, maybe.

G000044686

SURVIVING
THEIR LOVE

GREY WOLF

Surviving Their Love

This book was first published in Great Britain in paperback during October 2019.

The moral right of Grey Wolf is to be identified as the author of this work and has been asserted by him in accordance with the Copyright, Designs and Patents Act of 1988.

Email: ads2life@btinternet.com

ISBN: 9781702513524

DEDICATION

I would like to dedicate this book to the very special women whom I had the honour of sharing time within my life, you have taught me so much, and I am so grateful for all my memories both good and not so good. Each one you have certainly made impressions on my life. I have learned to love, and I have had some heartache also, I have loved and lost, and sometimes I thought I would never get up off my knees. The time I spent with you has been amazing. All of my experiences both good and bad, were all part of getting me to the man I am today. For those of you I hurt, I apologise from the bottom of my heart and I am truly sorry, For those of you who hurt me, I thank you, you have taught me great lessons, and I hope I have learned my lessons well. If any of you read this book, maybe you will have a better understanding of me and my behaviour, but know I loved you for sure, and the memories of our moments of that love are with me always. Life can be difficult sometimes, but I try to remember the good things and the good times we shared together, I loved you then and I always will, our relationships have changed but the love is always constant. To my best friend John, I thank you for always being there for me, you are the hardest working man I ever met, and one of the kindest, with a heart of gold and though we have had our differences from time to time, I want to thank you from the bottom of my heart, I love you my friend, thank you for your unconditional friendship and for always having my back...

To all the people in my life who watch over me now, new friends and old, and to a new friend who just came into my life recently. Thank you, Evelyn, for all your support and help. You are an inspiration, you have my love and respect. Thank you for your help in getting this book published, and for kicking my ass when I got lazy lol.

CHAPTER ONE

My name is Paul, but I'm also known as "Wolf." My full spiritual given name is "Grey Wolf The Spirit Warrior". I received this name in a Native American Ceremony, by a Native American Shaman. I have studied Shamanic healing and many other forms of healing; I have spent lots of time with Shamanic healers and learnt so much from them. The Native American way is with Respect and Honour, and I live my life by this code. I have many certifications in healing practices. But God/Great Spirit, does not do certification. we are all healers, it's just some of us practice more than others. All my friends call me "Wolf" and I am honoured to be called that. A Wolf protects his pack, family and friends. He is brave and loyal to his clan and would lay down his life for those he loves. Some of my Spirit Guides are wolves, and they guide and protect me. My path is the way of the warrior, and I have chosen to walk this path. We all choose our life path, we always have choices, so choose well, make changes where necessary, learn and teach well. You are the one in charge, it's your story, so live it well. EVERY PROBLEM HAS A SOLUTION, so find your solutions, and remember, THERE IS NO HEALING IN SECRETS.

The reason I have written this book is because I wanted to try to show people who have had experiences similar to mine, that you can make your life your own, you can make your life better, no matter what has happened to you. Too many times I have heard "my Father or my Mother, He/she did this or that, said this or that, made me feel, took away from me, made me do, I was helpless, they broke my trust", and much, much more.

When we were children that was possible, but now we are adults we are the people in control of what we do and say we are responsible for all our actions be they verbal or physical. So take control of yourself and make your life better, change the things that are hurting you, but first you must change your idea of you, and your thought processes that make you feel LESS THAN. Only you can do this, if you put your energy into making your life better and the lives of those who love and trust you, instead of destroying everything around you, it is possible to find your true reason for being here. You are the only power in your life, and only you, can make the difference between a happy peaceful life, and a life of hardship and misery. If you are not happy nobody around you will be either. I would like to try and suggest to you a new way, a way to walk happily on this planet with new ways of thinking, a new mindset, and a better, joyful, free feeling, that shows you your road and path to self contentment and peace. In this book you will read about my life and personal hardships. You will read about abuse, sorrow and loss, but this is a story of triumph and success. I hope you will empathise with some of my experiences and respond to the stimulation and courage.

The way of the warrior is not about fighting and killing, blood or guts, it is about honour and self respect. My path is about peace, kindness and gentleness, in a place where Honour, love, and respect seems to have disappeared. The way of the warrior is to love and protect, to help those who require it, and to lead with honour, respect and love, this is my way and the way of all great warriors gone before me. I want to teach you that fear is your only enemy, and you are worthy of a peaceful and loving life.

But first, we need to try to strip away all negative thoughts, and behaviours or anything that does not serve you or the good of the people who truly love you. We are all one spirit, coming from the same place we are all connected, what harm we do to others we also do to ourselves. So let's make the place where we are, into the place we want it to be, not a place where we do penance, to change your life you must change the way you act or behave and have some belief in yourself, and your own ability. Know you can be anything you want to be and do anything you want to do. you do not need degrees or diplomas. You are your own teacher, when we make mistakes, we learn, and this is the hard way!!! We don't need to make mistakes to learn, we need to trust our own intuition. We need to clear our minds of "dis-ease". Our paths are one of beauty, and we are blessed with all we need and could ever want. But we are lost in the belief we are missing something, and we need more, so we continue to be victims, believing we never got what we deserved, always missing out, and being hard done by. When something happens to someone else, we say they are either luckier than us, or they don't deserve it. We are not happy unless we can empathise with their bad luck or misfortune. So it seems that life is unfair. We come from two people who came from two other sets of people and so on backwards to all our ancestors, they were taught different things in different times, these teachings are taught to us by our parents, who learned from theirs, and some teachings are not relevant for us or our time, the conditioning we inherit is ridiculous, but the cycle goes on until we wake up and take control of our own minds, until we break cycles and begin to open our hearts and minds. I believe if you expect nothing, then everything received is a surprise. Even in defeat, we learn something, and our misfortune is due to the fact we are taught to believe we are not good enough to be fortunate enough! So we miss it. This lifetime is but a blink of the eye in terms of time and space. There are millions of years gone before and more that will come after us, it is testament to the fact that our time here, won't even make a ripple in time. So for the short time we are here, why not make it as happy as you can, remember, if you are not happy, no one around you will be!!! SO LETS START THERE!!! At the beginning with you, change your mind, and be happy.

CHAPTER TWO

To begin a book like this is difficult, so I think I will try from this direction. I am a 57 year old man, and I have studied many forms of religion. I was raised a Catholic, but as I grew, I understood this religion was not based in truth. I believe in Jesus Christ and his father (Great Spirit). I believe that Jesus was one of the greatest healers of our time. He was very special in that he believed in who he was. He taught many lessons right up until his death, and in death, he showed that the spirit (soul) lives on. We are all part of the same spirit; we are all connected. We are in Great Spirit, and Great Spirit is in all of us. We are one with everything. Spirit is energy and energy is everywhere so we are everywhere, think of yourself as a drop of water, when you die this single drop of water goes back to its source, so let's say that's an ocean, when the drop hits the water it becomes part of the whole again, it's not separate it's connected to everything, I like to think that's why our loved ones who have passed on are still with us because they are pure energy again, A LITTLE DROP THAT BECOMES AN OCEAN. To believe in yourself is sometimes very difficult when you were taught to believe something different, but believe you are the most important person in your life!!! This does not mean you do what you want, and it's all about you. The most important thing to remember, is we are all connected, so what you do, reflects on everyone and everything in your life. It's very easy to be angry, but it takes courage to be honest. When you are wrong admit it, and try to accept responsibility for your actions, then you make amends and heal the mind and the heart. We were taught that the trinity was God the father, Son and Holy Ghost, we are in fact the real trinity, we are MIND, BODY AND SPIRIT/SOUL, if any of this trinity is out of balance then we are in trouble, so it's important to take care of yourself, mind yourself, take time out to heal and restore your mind, body or spirit. When we are peaceful we function better, in any stressful situation we need to be calm. You need to have total control of yourself, your mind, your actions you are totally responsible for. Nobody can make you do what they want you too. Your decision is yours. Unfortunately, we are all bound in conditioning!

When we arrive into this life, we are perfect forms of Great Spirit. We are totally honest, when we need something, we let it be known, we cry, smile, and show we are here and command attention. There is nothing so beautiful as your baby, your child. We are here to love and protect their life, and hopefully teach this child to be the best they can be, and hopefully the best version of themselves as they grow into adulthood. We don't own our children; we only have a loan of them. Hopefully we teach them well, and set them free to live their lives. I was born in 1962, I lived in Fatima Mansions which is on the Southside of Dublin City. When I was 2 years old, we moved to Finglas which is on the outskirts of the North side of Dublin City. My big sister was two years older than me and even then she minded me. She was just a baby herself. We were always close, and we loved each other very much. My Mother was about 21 years old, and my Father was about 23 years old. My mother was blonde and very beautiful, my Dad was a dark haired man and very handsome, but he was a very angry man, and very possessive of my mother. I can remember shouting and fighting even then. So I grew up with noise, it became the norm. As I grew, I was told and taught to protect my sister, and as the other children came along I would protect them too. So if you hurt my brothers or sisters, you answered to me. One day my sister came in crying, some boy had hit her. So my father gave me a hammer to go and hit the boy with it. I was just going out the door, when my mother stopped me, and took the hammer from me, but my father sent me out anyway, I was maybe 4 or 5 years old. I hit the boy for hitting my sister, he never hit her again. I gained a bad reputation and had no friends. The local mothers were afraid that I would do something bad to their children. I remember many years later as an adult, a friend's mother said to me, "You were a little bastard, the kids and their parents were afraid of you, because you would hit them with anything that came to hand!" I loved this woman, she was a kind lady, and I spent many a day in my friend's home, the fact I had a crush on my friend's sister was another reason why I spent so much time there. One night when I was about fifteen, I sang outside her window, 'more than a woman' by the Bee Gee's. I never got to kiss her, but I did kiss her sister lol.

When I was about 2 years old my mother gave birth to my little sister, when she brought her home, from the hospital I didn't really like her, so apparently, I bit her big toe because "I was so jealous." So my Mother said, I don't remember so I am denying it. As a little boy I had no friends, because everyone was afraid of what I might do. I was taught to hit first, and ask questions later, to win at any cost. If I lost a fight, I had to go and fight again. As I grew up, I realised that if I wanted friends, I had to control myself. So I made friends with "John", he was my best friend when I was little up until my teenage years, until we went to secondary school, John and I had a great time together and would annoy anyone we could. John and I would spend a lot of time getting into mischief but his mum was a lovely lady, she was kind to me. John's Dad was an ex-soldier, he was strict, but fair, John was never beaten, but he was slapped and sent to bed. I on the other hand, had the shite kicked out of me, so we always tried not to get caught, we had a great time together, a real Batman and Robin team. We even cut up his mum's blankets because they were black, and we made capes out of them. Johns mum had just bought them, but she just laughed at us after telling us off.

As I got older, I didn't want to fight but my Dad would call me a sissy, I just wanted to play, I didn't want to hurt anyone. But if anyone hurt my sisters I would go after them. My relationship with my father was one of fear, I did not like or respect him, but I did love him, he was my Dad, my hero. He could understand what all the Indians were saying in the cowboy movies, so he would translate for us, we believed everything he said lol Sometimes he was kind, and would play with us, we would play fight on the floor with my brother and two sisters. I remember one time when we were coming home from Cork where we had been on holidays, and we were driving through the Phoenix park in Dublin late at night, my father said that the gates were closed and we would have to jump the gate in the car, he said our car was chitty chitty bang bang, so we all had to get down on the floor behind the seats and when we hit the cattle rumble strips he said we had landed and we could come out from behind the seats, we really believed him.

My brother was born when I was five. He was a lovely handsome little fella, I was delighted to have my brother, and I couldn't wait for him to grow, I watched over him and looked after him. So now I had 2 sisters and a brother to protect and I was only 5 years old. But hey! I was batman! so no problem. John and I got into all sorts of trouble, my brother was growing. My older sister took care of me if I got hurt, one day I was promised a kiss from a girl, if I could jump the river, now the river was full of shite n all sorts, a kiss was a kiss so I attempted the jump landing on my arse in the river covered in shit, my father was gonna kill me for sure and I was late going home, my father came looking for me so I hid, he and my mother were going out, so when they left I went home and my sister cleaned me up. I was about eight and she was ten, she tried to wash my clothes so I wouldn't get into trouble, but she got her hand caught in the mangle on the machine and needed stitches, so my father beat the shit outa me, but she tried to save me, she always did. I had a younger sister who I watched over, and my little brother. I loved them so much and would never let anyone hurt them. I was told to love them by my mother, and to protect them by my father. Little did I know, I would have to protect them from him.

My father was put into an industrial school in Cork when he was very young, he was wild as a child and his father beat the living daylights out of him. Eventually my father was put in the school where he suffered mental, physical and sexual abuse. He was 8 years old when he was put in there and he was 13 years old when he came out. My father was a very angry man, he beat all of us, including my mother. He had no self control, and wouldn't stop until we couldn't get up, he would beat us so badly that sometimes it would take forever to heal. We were his babies, he was supposed to love and protect us, not half kill us. My mother on the other hand was a very selfish woman, I truly believe, we were sacrificed to my father's anger, so she didn't get beaten. My mother knew what was going on and did nothing. If we did, or said, anything wrong, she would always say 'I'm tellin' your father!' and she would tell him when he got home from work and we would be beaten. My mother never hit us. that was my father's job.

CHAPTER THREE

My first experience I can remember of my father's anger and violence was, when I was about 2 years old. We were going to the shop my sister and myself, with my father. As a child I was running ahead, he was shouting at me to stop running, I ran and fell into a hole with broken glass in it, and I got a very deep cut on my left thigh, my father slapped me very hard and dragged me home. The wound needed stitches, but because my mother was expecting my little sister, he would not take me to the hospital, my father just bandaged me himself and sent me to bed "for being Bold. "I still have the scar at the top of my thigh. Not only was I hurt, I was slapped and punished. My father didn't pull his punches, he would say, "This is gonna hurt me more than you." So then he would beat the shite out of us. My father hit us as if we were men, we tried to avoid upsetting him, but he got upset very easily. One day I spoke as I passed the living room door while he was watching "Match of the Day" on TV. The living room door opened, and I was sent down the hallway on my arse, with the clatter he gave me. My father was a very aggressive man, he would kick and punch and use anything that came to hand to hurt us.

As a child, I was physically, sexually and mentally abused, but I blocked out the sexual abuse for years, because what came in the night wasn't nice and it terrified me, I spent most of my childhood in fear, If something happened, my sisters and brothers were lined up in the living room, he would ask "who did it?" already knowing the answer, then he would beat us so badly. I would try to protect my brothers and sisters, so I would always say it was me who did it, he would the beat the living life out of me, while the others watched. When he was done with me, he would ask the others again "Who did it?" then he would beat them. so nearly always, two of us got beaten, and on it went. I tried to protect them, but he would always beat us anyway. Sometimes my older sister would speak up, then she would be beaten first. She tried to save me from my father's anger only to get beaten herself.

As a child I would do impressions and sing for my brothers and sisters, because they were so afraid, but this would infuriate my father, so we would all get punished. He would turn off the landing light and leave us in the pitch black, but we would still laugh and giggle. Both my sisters would come into my bed and get in behind me, my brother was on the top bunk, I would sing them to sleep. when we were all together, we were safe, or at least we thought so. The girls used to come to my bed often because they were so afraid. I thought I could protect them, but what I didn't understand for many years was who and what I was protecting them from, they were protected because when they were behind me, my father didn't come for them. I used to get so annoyed sometimes with my sisters, but they were my little sisters, even though I wasn't the eldest. My eldest sister went to live with my aunt, and I went to my Gran's for a while, but the others were left with our father, my youngest sister had no protection and she never forgave me. One day she was very angry with me and she told me that I had left her to him. She said I didn't protect her, and I didn't care about her.

We were never safe. I would try to protect them from my Father, and I did my best, but I would get annoyed because there was three of us in my single bed. I knew my sisters were scared, so I put up with it. We loved each other so much, and besides, my dad said I was to protect them always. Little did I know what was really going on. The violence was the norm in our home, so we just lived that way, always afraid and looking out for each other. I learned to stay out of my dad's way as much as I could, I always tried not to get caught. But my mother would always tell stories to him about us, so we would get it from him when he came home from work.

One day I wouldn't eat my vegetables, one reason was, I don't like sprouts, my father grew his own vegetables and my mother was a terrible cook, so when he came home from work she told him I didn't eat my sprouts, my dinner was cold so he sat me in a bath full of cold water in my clothes, and fed me the sprouts. I was retching and throwing up, but he made me eat it all, then he gave me a hiding and sent me to bed. I hurt all over, I don't know what drove this man to want to hurt us so much, I always loved him and craved his praise or admiration.

But not a hope in hell was I going to get it, I could never do anything right and he never failed to tell me that, mind you, this made me more determined. It's hard to understand but a child that is abused doesn't hate their parents, they hate themselves, I just pushed myself harder. My mother always told me to protect my brother and sisters, and to love my siblings, and I did with all of me.

CHAPTER FOUR

When we are children, we are taught our conditioning. This conditioning is based on the beliefs of our parents, we learn from them and they have some fucked up ideas about life, but they say they know best and we believe them. I remember one time, I heard my mother speak about and aunt of mine. She said, she didn't like this woman, so one day when my aunt was in my home, I said, "My mammy doesn't like you!" My mother nearly fell through the floor! I was told to be quiet, my mother started to explain to my aunt that I was only a child, and didn't understand what I was saying, I was only four or five years of age. I only spoke what was true, and what she said, but now I was not a good boy for what I had just said. I was punished for that too. Now the conditioning was, don't speak the truth or you will have problems, 'Little children should be seen and not heard!' I am sure we all know that expression. what is being said is, children are not important, but of course this is not true, because one day, the children grow up to be adults.

When we grow into adulthood with the impression you are not valid, and what you think is unimportant, how can you be an asset to yourself, your family and your community. In today's society children have very little respect for anything, or anyone. Their parents teach them to be selfish and disrespectful. Because we want to make up for the hurt we feel, or felt when we were children we give them everything that is possible, no matter what the cost, and now nothing has any value.

For myself, I believe, when you work for something, and you make an effort, it is of a much more important value to you. We need to teach our children to respect everyone and everything. I practice Shamanism as a way of life, I am a healer and I believe totally, that everything is connected, we must respect each other and everything.

Protecting my siblings and mother came at a physical cost to me from my father, I had to step up many times. I pulled my father off my mother, only to be beaten myself, he used intimidation and brutality, he had no soul. He didn't seem to care what damage he did. I learned to respect the fear, but I never respected him. He would hit us with whatever came to hand. One day he beat me for about 30 minutes, I was so badly beaten, I ended up in bed for a week to heal. I was giving my aunt a bucket of coal, as they were very cold and didn't have much money, my father told me not to do it, but I wanted to help my aunt. She lived next door to us, so I went over the back wall and filled the bucket with coal, as I came back over the wall, I put the bucket on the wall. my father was standing with his back to the wall, so when I popped my head over, my father grabbed me by the throat, and dragged me off the wall, I hit the ground with a thud, he started to kick me, Before I got a chance to run. He beat the living daylights out of me. He used stair rods, frying pan, football boots, feet, fists, and a leather belt. I was kicked up and down the hall, I actually peed myself by the front door. He beat me up the stairs and into my bedroom, were he told me too take off my pants, as he opened his, I said "No!" and wrapped myself in the blanket. That was the last thing I remember; I was knocked unconscious. This is the reason I called this book, "Surviving Their Love." He loved me so much he wanted to kill me.

My mother drummed it into us kids that we were to love, lookout for, protect and care for each other, and we did. I loved my sisters and little brother, they were beautiful. My eldest sister was so kind, she took care of us she would mind us when our parents went out. She would get us dressed and ready for school, she made our lunches and sent us off. We went to school on our own, when my younger brother and sister were going to school, my sister and I would bring them. We really loved each other dearly, and to this day my oldest sister is our rock. She suffered so much at the hands of my parents, they both hurt her. I believe that my mother was jealous of my sisters, she knew what was happening to them and did absolutely nothing. My younger sister also went through hell, as did my brothers, my mother had another baby when I was eleven, this boy was my father's blue-eyed boy. He got everything we didn't, and he would rat us out to our father, I didn't like him at all. But I protected him as he was my brother. When my father would line us up, and ask who did it, he would tell on us, so we would be beaten. I sometimes wanted to choke him, but he was only a baby, as he grew, I think he got the idea of my father. It was only in his late teens, they bounced of each other. My other brother was my mother favourite, but he was a good kid, we nearly lost him when he was hit by a car, and ended up in hospital with a broken leg and other severe injuries, but he loved me his big brother, and got me a date with one of the nurses! charming little fucker!!

As we grew up, the abuse never stopped. Many times, I would try to stop my father from hurting my siblings, and I got a hiding for it and then he would turn on them. The abuse depended on what happened in his day, if someone upset him at work, we paid for it. If the house wasn't clean, we got it. My older sister and I were often kept home from school to clean the house, as my mother would be 'too tired' to do it. My older sister would get us ready and send us to school, she would stay home and clean the house from top to bottom, she would get food ready for us coming home, a day or so later it would be my turn to do it. Back then the school inspector would call to houses if you missed too much school, and you would be put into care. We would see the inspector knocking on doors, and we would be scared they were coming for us. My mother used to say, "If you love me, you will clean the house." The emotional blackmail always worked. She would get me out of bed some nights at two or three in the morning, just to rub her head and massage her feet because she was tired after coming in from work. She worked part time in a factory, not far from where we lived.

I hated doing that for her, her feet would smell, and she smoked. With the mixture of sweat and smoke I always felt sick, to this day I hate cigarettes, and women's nylon tights. She would tell me I was the best, and if I loved her I would do it.

My mother is the most selfish person I know, she would share our sweets and hide her own. But I loved her and always took care of her. As a child and as I grew up my relationship with my mother was very loving. I would have died for her, and nearly did on one occasion. I was a good son. When I got older, I worked hard, I had my own car, I always had sweets in my car and she knew that. She would say "I am dying for a sweet." So I would give her what sweets I had. I started working in a supermarket in Finglas part time, when I was twelve years old. I earned twenty five pence and hour, I worked four hours, Thursday and Friday, and eight hours on Saturdays. So I earned four pounds. My mother took two pounds, I kept two pounds, I saved one pound and spent the other one. Life was good lol. I had also just started secondary school in the Patrician Brothers in Finglas, my friends went to the tech school. I was going to college according to my mother, but my history in school was not great, so I wasn't expecting bells and whistles. I hated authority, and now I was with the Christian Brothers. When I was in primary school, we had the hardest teacher for our fifth and sixth year class. This teacher was hardcore. I was always in trouble, the teacher had a bamboo type cane, he would use it to leather the shit out of us. He would be sweating from the energy he put into hitting us with that cane, the fecking thing was curved, it was used that much. I was never afraid of being hit by him; I was well used to it. It used to frustrate the hell out of him I wouldn't cry as the other boys did. When he would hit me, he would say, "This is for your benefit." Now where did I hear that before?

I would stand there, and he would push me around to provoke a reaction, and then he would tell me to hold out my hand and he would let fly with the cane, I would never flinch, he would swing the cane from behind his head and whack the hands of us. One day I got into a fight in class with one of the other boys, who was just a bully (I hate bullies) my friend Davy and I would protect our corner and would play fight the other guys. but this one guy got very rough with Davy and hurt him. My protective instinct kicked in, everyone was afraid of this kid, he was a little crazy. I stepped up and we fought, I knocked the shit out of him for hurting my friend. The teacher walked in while I was choking this kid and grabbed me by the scruff of the neck and flung me across the room, I was only about eleven years old. He stood the two of us at the top of the class, he asked what was going on and neither of us answered. He went to his desk and took out the cane, After the first twelve whacks across my hands he was furious, I didn't blink, the other lad nearly lost an ear trying to avoid getting hit, he kept pulling his hand away, but he still got his twelve slaps, then it was back to me again, another twelve, the sweat was pumping from the teacher and my hand was on fire but I didn't flinch. I was in so much pain. I wanted to say "stop! enough!" But in my mind that was weak, and I was not going to give that fucker the pleasure of seeing me cry, so I got my second twelve whacks. The other poor lad was crying and squirming all over the place, but he still got his slaps as well. I thought it was over, I was weak with the pain, I just wanted to sit down, but no! that was not gonna happen. The teacher got on the intercom to the headmaster and we were sent to his office. Off we marched together not a word spoken between us. In the headmaster's office we were given a choice of which cane we wanted to be hit with, he had a about six canes to choose from. We had just been hit with a skinny one, my hands were sore and raw. So I chose the thick one, it hurt just as much, after twelve more slaps I nearly passed out. But the other poor fucker was being chased around the office, I thought it was funny, I thought the headmaster might have a heart attack if we were lucky. On the way back to class, I told the other boy that I would see him after school, but we were both too sore to fight again, so it didn't happen. But when I got home, my father was told what had happened at school, and he gave me another beating. The guy I was fighting met my brother a few years ago and told him, your brother was one tough bastard, we are both in our fifties, but he too clearly remembered that day. It was an experience we won't forget.

CHAPTER FIVE

In our lifetime, we learn many lessons. Every person who comes into our lives is a teacher or a pupil, we need to learn to listen and respect what they have to say, some of the best teachers in my life were the women in my life. In life you need balance, and women taught me some feminine balance. There have been many women, and I thank them all. But the few women who had the courage to stay a while, you have my total respect. The first woman in my life, was my mother. I loved her so much, and when I knew she lied to me and did not protect me, my love changed for her. She sent me to my grandmothers to live, because she knew my father would kill me. He had beaten me so many times and maybe one time might be one time too many, so I was sent away to protect him.

When I was about six or seven, I stared to wet the bed, this made my father crazy. He would embarrass me, as much as possible. I remember we were on holiday and he told the lady who owned the bed n breakfast that I was a pisser, and she needed to cover the bed I was sleeping in. I wanted the ground to open up and swallow me. My mother always made sure I was clean and didn't smell. A boy in my class always smelt of pee, and I would have died if anyone knew about me. But my father was not so kind.

I lived with my grandmother on and off, this was the woman who taught me to love, she was my friend, and we talked about everything. I loved her so much, she was so gentle and kind, always affectionate and loving, she was a great cook too, so I loved staying with her and I was safe and relaxed for a while. I remember the time I realised I loved her more than I did my mother. At the time I was very sad, I felt I had betrayed my mother for having those feelings. My grandmother was a very important part of my life. When she died, I was eighteen, and a part of me died also. I lost my best friend, she told me to marry my first wife Marie. My grandmother was very wise, Marie was my best friend, and I loved her very much. At around twelve years old I was working part time and had little money, but I was happy. Because between school, and training, working weekends, karate and football on Sundays, I was really busy, so I wasn't home much. I went to bed early most nights and I had very little contact with my father. So life was relatively good. I was always chasing girls, busy, busy man, but still I found time to piss my father off. I could do it just by turning up.

Living with my grandmother was great except when my uncle came to stay, because of him I wasn't even safe there. I suffered abuse from my mother's brother, he beat me up and always belittled me when he could, he was an asshole, a champion boxer in the RAF, an all-Ireland champion in the nineteen sixties, a real piece of shit. My mother's other brother was the same, but he did take me under his wing for a while, he had no sons, he was all about control and manipulation. When I stood up for myself, he turned his back on me and wouldn't speak to me for years. These two men had their own agenda, one brother taught me to box, by letting bigger guys knock the shit out of me. He would then tell me how useless I was, but I could take a punch. The other built my body by torturing me and doing things my body couldn't handle, but I did get strong and learn how to fight. This all went on from when I was four years old until I was twelve. To this day my mother talks about her great brothers, but they were child abusers and wife beaters, and neither of them would stand up for us against my father and he was a coward. In secondary school life didn't get any better for me, the Christian Brothers were very angry men. One was gay I think, but back then I didn't know what 'gay' was. He used to touch us all the time, he would get us to write on the black board and when he gave us the chalk, he would pat us on the bum as we passed. Then he would squeeze behind us between the desk and blackboard and rub against us. The other Christian Brother used to beat the crap out of us if we did something wrong.

One day a big guy hit my friend, we were in our first year of secondary school, so I was only twelve, my friend was different, he was gentle, and afraid of confrontation, he was gay, although as I have said, I didn't understand what it was or meant, all I knew was he was my friend,. The big guy hit my friend; I told the guy not to touch my friend again. This guy was huge, he picked me up and threw me over the bicycle rack. I landed on my hands and knees and hurt my back when I hit the bike rack, I got up and went to town on the guy. I had him on the ground punching him, when someone started hitting me with a belt from behind, I jumped up and turned and punched him, I didn't realise it was one of the Brothers. "Oh shit!" I thought I'm in for it now. I was dragged into the office and I got a beating. I was told to get my mother and father to come to a meeting in the school, I was so scared of telling my father, I tried to put off telling him for as long as I could, but eventually on the threat of expulsion, I told my mother. Of course, my mother told my father, and I waited for the beating, but it didn't happen. Well this was a new one!!! My father asked me what happened, so I told him. He said I had better not be lying to him, I was so scared of my father, the day came for the meeting, I was in class, my stomach was sick, then the call came for me to go to the office, when I walked in there were four Brothers, my mother and father, I nearly passed out.

My father asked, "Where is the other boy?" He wanted to see him. So the Brothers sent for him, when he walked in he was nearly as big as my father. My father looked at me and asked, "Is this the boy you fought with?" I said "Yes." He asked the boy, if I fought him and beat him, the boy said "yes." My father then let fly, he told the Brothers what he thought of them, he grabbed the Brother that hit me by the throat and told him, if he ever put a hand on me again and he would kill him. He told the head Brother, if he expelled me, he would come for him and burn the school down, he told them all how much he hated them. I was in total shock! This was the first and only time that my father stood up for me, "My father loves me! Wow!" I was so proud he protected me, so fuck you all! The real reason he went ballistic, was because he was in that industrial school in Cork, and the Christian Brothers there, had abused him. So his anger and outburst was because of himself, and not me. I found that out many years later. On the day in question, I was told not to cause any more problems, but at least I didn't get a beating.

I hated school, and got into more trouble with the Brothers, I told my mother, but she never told my father, she was afraid he would get into trouble or get arrested. For my mother, my father came first, she definitely cared more about him than us. At home each one of us was suffering, my siblings were having a really hard time at the hands of my father, he really hurt them. In later years I was to learn the real story. My father would belittle us any chance he got, I began to skip school, and cause a lot of problems. as I said, I was working, and at fourteen, I was offered an apprenticeship as a butcher. I had been in the supermarket two years now. So I left school and took the job.

Shit was still going on at home, we were always afraid, but I was making money now, so I could move out. I tried not to go home much, I had my first serious girlfriend, so I was with her a lot, I stayed over at my grandmothers whenever I could, or with my friends. My mother took my wages every week and took half my money. I was earning nineteen pounds a week; she took ten pounds. She always complained about not having any money, and how we were struggling, my oldest sister was working too, my mother took half her money from her too, so my mother was doing okay. Through all those years, I didn't remember the sexual abuse, - that was to come later, but the mental and physical abuse was as strong as ever I hated living at home, always worried and scared, never knowing when the shit would hit the fan.

When we were little my mother would leave us alone with my father to clean the house, as I said my oldest sister was like a mammy to us, she looked after us, and she had her own troubles I just didn't realise how bad she was having it. My mother would go into Dublin City every Saturday to get shopping, this went on for as long as I can remember. So every Saturday, my sisters and I would clean the house from top to bottom. My father, used to sit me on the head of the brush with a cloth wrapped around it, and used it to polish the floors, the others would be polishing the furniture, changing beds, and doing everything else. we would have to stand outside on the window ledges to clean the windows, even though we were scared of heights. I always did the outside of the windows so my sisters wouldn't fall. At around six o'clock my mother would return, we would all be bathed, and then have a fry up for tea. we would get to watch a little TV, and then into bed, if we were lucky, we were left alone. Other days my mother would go to her friends as often as she could and leave us alone. Many times, after school she would be at her friends, and it was my sister who looked after us. My mother has admitted that she knew what my father was doing, but she could do nothing about it, and so she did nothing. Please remember for me all this stuff was normal, all the violence, and fear, looking after ourselves, all of this was our norm and we knew nothing different. These situations were in our lives from the start, so it was the way it was. It has affected each one of us differently. we are all trying to cope with the aftermath. I put pen to paper, not because I had a hard time. I wrote this because I know we were not the only children to go through this. My father was an animal, who blamed everybody else for his behaviour. He gave me, "it happened to me" bullshit. I believe we are all responsible for the things we do and say, and learned behaviour is a natural course for many people. I would like people to understand, everything you do is your decision. If you are an asshole, it's not your father's fault, it's your decision, you are being you. I have worked with many people who have these issues, and they feel they are owed something, we are owed nothing, my mother always said that we owed her because she brought us into this world, like we had asked for it.

My youngest brother is a drug addict, he blames me and my father, mother, brother, sisters for the way he is. My mother supports this, but he was the one who's choice it was to put the needle in his arm. He suffered a huge loss in his life when he was young, he lost his beautiful little girl to cot death, the little angel went to sleep and never woke up, and instead of honouring her, he chooses to blame. He has hurt so many people in his life including strangers, and it's not his fault!? So tell me, who put the gun in his hand? who told him to hurt people? He made his own choices. As I have pointed out, we all came from the same place, we all make our own decisions we are responsible for our decisions. **It begins and ends with you**. Every thought in your head is your own thought, you decide right and wrong, **you are the power in your life**. So be just that and use your power for good. Be kind and loving. It's up to you, but start with you. I was working at the supermarket for a few years, I was in my third year, and had learned well. One butcher took me under his wing, I was not quite seventeen, and was doing the work of two men. Butchering was a trade, but a hard one. Sometimes you would be in the fridge for hours freezing your ass off. I had a major problem with a charge hand, he was a right prick, so we bounced off each other. One day it came to a head, because I saw him take a back hander from a meat supplier, he then did his best to get me fired. So one day I just left. To be honest I thought he was paying for the meat, it wasn't till later when he was sacked for taking the money, I understood it.

CHAPTER SIX

As a child living with my grandmother, I used to go to the local butcher with a note from her for the meat she wanted, I wasn't big enough to reach the counter as I was only a little fella, I would give the note to Mr Ryan and only Mr Ryan because my grandmother told me too. When I left my job in the supermarket, I went to Mr Ryan and asked him for a job, he remembered who I was, and started me straight away with work. My first pay packet he paid me a proper butchers wage, he said I was as good as any butcher he knew. He saw I was delighted, one hundred and eleven pounds! The previous week I was on only thirty nine pounds a week, and now here I was being paid a man's wage, this was more than my father earned. when I got home my mother took half my wages. I didn't care I still had twice as much as I ever had, and a little more! I gave my mother and extra twenty pounds to go and buy a coat she wanted, I felt I was loaded. Shortly after that I met my first wife, and I bought a car, my father wasn't happy with me and gave me a hard time.

When I was sixteen, I wanted to move out of the house, this was because I wanted to buy a motorbike. My father said if I bought a motorbike he would burn it. I was so sick and tired of his bullying. So I told my mother I wanted to move out, she said I couldn't leave her, or my brothers and sisters

alone with my father. and even more than that, I had to protect them,
Because I love them so much I stayed home. I was getting bigger and
stronger, and for me my Father's day was coming. I had made a promise to
my mother and I had always kept my promises. One day I was home for
lunch I was just about eighteen years old, my little brother was home for
lunch too. My mother was home and my father arrived in while we were
eating. My brother and I were most likely teasing my mother as we were
always laughing and happy together. For some reason my father decided to
start on me. He asked me if I was a big man, a tough guy, I said I had no
idea what his problem was, but he was spoiling for a fight. I seemed to be
what was fuelling his anger, I got up to leave, he was calling me a coward,
as I was leaving my mother was pushing me out of the door, she said,
"Remember your promise." I just walked away, he was giving me dogs
abuse, I had no Idea what was going on, as I got to the top of the cul-de-
sac were we lived, my little brother came running after me, he was upset
and crying. he had just been clattered, the poor little chap, He was frantic,
he said, "He's killing mammy!" I ran straight back to the house and into the
kitchen, where my father had my mother on the kitchen table with a knife
to her throat. So I ran at him and took him out through the back door on his
arse, before he got back up, I grabbed my mother and pushed her out of the
kitchen, she came back in and held my hands while my father punched me,
he slammed my head into the wall a few times as I tried to protect my
mother, but my mother stopped me from hitting my father and always
reminded me of my promise. I had a black eye going back to work, my
boss asked what happened, and I told him. He said I was to go with him
that evening. I was dating my first wife at the time, so we picked her up in
his Jag, he and his wife took us to dinner, me sitting there with a nice
shiner, when my girlfriend asked what happened, I just said I did it at work.

I couldn't say my father gave me a black eye. The reason it all happened
was because my mother provoked my father about work, saying her son
was making more money than him, that's why he had a go at me. My
mother always protected my father, a few days later my mother came to me
to apologise for what my father did, I told her to tell him to stick it, and
said "If he ever touched to me again I would kill him." when I was buying

my first car again my father tried to stop me, but I bought it anyway. Just like when I was sixteen and wanted to buy a motor bike, Although I had no licence, but that was being sorted. I asked my father to collect my car for me and bring it home, he left it for two weeks, so I went and got it myself, I still wasn't eighteen, but I had my own car.

My car gave me so much freedom, I had a beautiful girlfriend, she was so pretty, and I loved her so much. We spent every moment we could together. My sister had a boyfriend. So the four of us would go away for weekends, We were free! I stood up to my father to protect my brothers and sisters, I was getting bigger and stronger, and he knew it, so the beatings stopped. I could fight back now, but my mother held me to my promise.

I was making good money, working for Mr. Ryan, and he was so kind to me, we also became great friends, and I loved him dearly. I got married a couple of years later, so my life was good. I would go home often to make sure my father was behaving himself, we developed some sort of friendship, but that was just to keep me on side. Behind it all he was still carrying on, but the others were too afraid to tell me. One evening I went to my mother's house after work, my father was in bed, my mother and I were talking, when a knock came to the door, it was the Gardai, my brother was in the station, so I went to get him. My father turned up at the station like a lunatic, the Garda and I spoke to him. I put my brother in the car and took him home, I told him that my father was going to give him a few thumps, but I would stop him if he went too far, and this I did. My father went nuts, I had to pull him off my brother I stood in front of him and wouldn't let my father hurt him, so my father went for a rope, he was going to hang my brother. I got my brother upstairs and I stood at the bottom of the stairs. I would not let my father pass, I was twenty one now, my brother was only sixteen, my father was forty two. My mother reminded me of my promise, but no way was I letting my father past me. I stayed there for hours, and when my father fell asleep, I took my brother home with me for the night. All my life I stood between my father and my family, and I thought I did a good job. But he was much cleverer than that, my family really suffered at his hands, and my mother is not blameless. For many years I didn't understand or remember the full extent of my father's behaviour.

My father was a very hard worker, he would do anything to make money, I never remember being hungry, and all our clothes were the best money could buy. We wore duffle coats, Clarks shoes, which we got fitted for. There was always plenty of food to eat. We had toys at Christmas, we had all we could need materialistically, our house was warm we always had animals, so from the outside we were very lucky. But in our home we lived in fear. My father was a great man to our neighbours, always kind and helpful. He had many affairs, according to my mother he was 'a whore master.' I saw him with another woman once, but she was friends with my mother, so I thought nothing of it, the two couples used to hang out together, so they were all friends as far as I knew. my mother told me I had betrayed her and I knew my father was having affairs.

In later years I learnt that my father had made passes at my two wives, and one or two other girlfriends of mine. My first wife and I lived with my parents for a few months while we waited for our new house to be ready. My wife was beautiful and worked as a nurse. My father passed by the hospital she worked in every morning, so he would take her to work, and I would pick her up in the evening. As She did eight AM to eight PM shifts and I finished work at 6PM, I was in plenty of time to collect her. When my father took my wife to work, he tried to talk her into having sex with him, but she never told me until after my father's death, because she knew I would kill him, I owed this lady so much, She loved me even when I was broken. She used to say, "When is my Paul coming back?" But I never made it home!!! One time she asked me to try again, to get back together and try to fix things. I loved her so much, but I had hurt her so badly. I didn't trust myself and I knew I would have hurt her again. I felt I wasn't good enough for her, she had suffered enough, I thought I was protecting her from me, I was not a good man, I was having affairs with many women, I always had three or four women on the go. Affairs were safe as there was no commitment. So many women came and went.

I was now a personal trainer, so I was fit and strong, and women were on tap. my mother called me 'a whore master. ' She used to say 'all men are bastards. ' I was a total bastard with other women, but I always looked after my wife and the children, she never wanted for anything.

My relationship with my mother totally changed the day I found out about the sexual abuse. The day my sister confirmed it, is the day I broke. I was devastated. I knew a cousin had been sexually abused by an aunt and her boyfriend, she was also abused by an uncle, the same uncle that beat me. The day I found out that my two beautiful sisters were abused, I just felt something break inside me, I felt I had been hit by a truck, all the air left my lungs, I just couldn't breathe. I burst into tears, and I looked at my sister who I loved so much, this girl I thought I was protecting all my life, and here I was, helpless, I couldn't save her. She had endured so much and never told me. I asked about my younger sister, she too had suffered at his hands. I was on my knees, absolutely floored, I was going to kill this man. I thought it was my uncle, but it was my father. I was devastated, she asked me not to say, or do anything. I left her house and I have no idea how I got home. I went and confronted my mother who had lied to me for so many years, I was devastated by her betrayal I couldn't even look at her and she did what she always did and played helpless. The years past and secrets were kept, the stress was unbearable, I cracked, actually, I broke down. My life fell apart, I would not let my parents near my children. One time I did bring the kids around to my mothers, but I never left them alone with my parents, not for one minute.

One day we went to my parents' house in the country. My son was running around chasing the chickens my parents had, and my father let a roar at him and said he would give my son a hiding if he didn't stop running in to the house. I stood up and told my father, if he even thought about putting a hand on my child, I would beat him to death and hand him his heart before he died. At that time, my father had no idea that I knew all about what he had done to my sisters. I went into the kitchen to get my wife and daughter; my daughter was sitting at the table eating a piece of cake and my mother was smoking. I had asked my mother not to smoke around my children, but as usual she just ignored me. I asked my wife to get my children's coats, when she went out of the room, I let my mother have it, my father came in and said it was their house and they could smoke if they wanted to. I replied that they had no respect and told them to fuck their home, they never saw my children again.

My parents used to give me such a hard time because I took care of Rie and the kids, they told me I was an idiot because I was working two jobs, twenty hours a day, for five days a week. I was taking care of two places and wanted to provide for my wife and children, so I worked hard and never asked anyone for anything. My mother would say my wife was lazy, staying at home all day sitting on her ass, while I was busting mine. I told her to mind her own business. My father would say, "What the fuck are you doing, giving her all your money!?"

I would say, "Did I ask you for money or help!? No!! it's not your money, mind your own business!" Even then, I was getting it wrong, as far as he was concerned. My mother once said to me, that until I started dating my wife, it was she who I would spend my money on, buying her gifts and flowers, and when that 'bitch' {Rie} came along, I gave it all to my wife. I told her it was my father's job to look after her, and I would always look after my wife. She was so jealous of my wife.

CHAPTER SEVEN

For a long time, I never understood why I did not accept love in my life, Rie came to me and always had the best intentions to help me. She loved me unconditionally and gave me the best gifts anyone could have given me, - she gave me my two children!! This woman was the most precious gift I had, and my life is so much better because she came into it. I have learnt many lessons in my life, but some of the most important she taught me. I caused this woman a lot of pain and hurt, and she never saw me coming, my heart was broken and even she could not help me. I was never violent towards her, but I did have an affair, and it broke her heart, I left her when our children were young, but I never abandoned them, I have always provided for them, and I am always beside them. we had a great relationship. I am so sorry Rie was so hurt, and if it was possible to take the hurt from her, I would do so in a second. I wanted my children and Rie to be safe, but at that time I was selfish, and a total bastard, I did not want Rie or the children to have any fear of me, worrying what would happen when daddy came home as I would never hurt them, so I left. At this time, I was very violent, and I couldn't control it, I was ready to die, and this is what I wanted. I had an affair as the girl gave me a lot of attention, I needed to break away, I did not believe in the family. Because of what I had found out, my mother lied and my father was a total sick bastard. When I was young I was taught that the family was all that was important. Tell the truth, take care, and protect your family, love and honour them, but I found out it was all a lie, and it broke me. I felt everything was a lie, my mother whom I trusted and adored, had lied to me, I asked if there was sexual abuse in my family, she told me No, and what sort of a person was I to ask such a thing! But something inside me was screaming out, So I began to look into it. My mother always told me to tell the truth, which I did, and got my ass kicked for it. She knew from an early age we were being abused and she did nothing. She had three brothers who were the most violent men I knew, they were always fighting, and were violent to their own families, I asked why nobody tried to help us, and I was told that her brothers would go to jail. I asked why we were not worth anything? for them to allow little children to be abused so badly, it shows the kind of cowards they were. All my life I never saw my father fight another man, he would roar and shout, but was never physical. He was a bully and a coward, When I understood that the sexual abuse had taken place, I lost it, and I wanted to kill my uncle and my father. I wanted to die, and I did my best to make it happen, my life became very violent, and the rage took over. The only sanity I found was, with my wife and my children. So, I couldn't commit suicide, as that would adversely affect my children. I didn't want my children to have to carry the burden of my suicide or live with the stigma attached to it. But if I died in a fight, that would be better, so I chose that road. My sisters asked me not to do anything, and not to make problems, So I promised to keep their secret. For me in this time, I believed in nothing and no one, I fought at every opportunity. One time I fought four guys, and I fought hard and beat them. there were lumps out of me, but I didn't care and pain was familiar, I slept maybe two hours every night, and I sat and watched my children sleeping until the sun came up. I had a great fear inside me that the devil was going to take my children. So I would sleep when the day broke. I wanted to end it all so badly, one day when a guy put a shotgun to my chest and said he was going to blow a hole in my chest, I told him shoot me, "Pull the trigger!" The guy was so surprised, and I got time to disarm him. The same guy is dead now, he was a junkie, so in reality he could have killed me that day. People who were there that day said I was a brave man, but in truth I would not let anyone intimidate me I wanted to die. I was scared and very frightened that day and afterwards I nearly passed out. Also at that time I didn't understand that I was having a nervous breakdown. My family did not help, my mother kept saying everything would be okay. I explained my fears and the reasons for them, but the secrets had to be kept. She knew what was happening but did nothing to help me. My mother had a nervous breakdown, her sister and two brothers did also. When I was younger, I saved my uncles life twice when he tried to kill himself. My mother knew what was happening with me, and why. For me, my life was falling apart, when I was younger I had it all, I was very sensible, and I always took care of any problems, when my family needed me, I was there. I provided money, and they always had my support. When I was on my knees I still had to keep the family secrets. I believe my mother didn't help me because I would have spoken to a doctor about what I knew. These secrets had to be kept, even if I lost my sanity, it was a small price to pay. But for me I was losing everything, my home, my wife, my children, my whole life. I was absolutely crazy In this time, and willing to fight and die if necessary, no one who challenged me got a chance to walk away, If you started an argument with me, you had to finish it.

I would like to speak about some of the things that made an impression on me, For me, it was a natural when I was a young boy to have fear of my father, if he was angry or tired you had to be careful with what you said or did. Every Saturday he played football, he was a very good but dirty player, he always said he was good but fair. He told me when he was younger he had trials with Manchester United, but he had to come home because my mother was pregnant on me, he blamed me because he had to come home, he told me I was the reason why he never made it and got famous, The truth was my mother was pregnant, and she wanted to live in Ireland, she was nineteen, this was a big problem back then, as she had my sister when she was seventeen, and me when she was nineteen. So she had to be pregnant at sixteen and un married, so he had to come home, they were married when she was seventeen, he was nineteen, She denies this, but this is the reasonable explanation, or else we were adopted which I know is not true. My mother had so many secrets, and we always had to play happy families. Anyway, when my father watched football on Sundays, we were not allowed to make noise. He would sit by the fire and eat dinner, if we made any noise we were in big trouble. My father always had the best to eat, I never saw my father drink alcohol. We always had good food on the table, and he did provide as well as he could for us. I sometimes think, he loved us, but he very seldom showed it. My life as a child was normal for me, it was all I knew. I didn't know it was wrong to beat your children so much, and for us to live in so much fear. Every moment for us was normal. As a child I believed my father was Superman, and he feared nothing. I looked up to him, I thought he was a good man, on the outside he was, everyone liked my father, He was a 'gentleman,' to neighbours and friends, but in the home he was a different animal. When I look back, I cannot believe the things he did, and why he was so brutal towards us. For me, a man takes care of his family, and I know I would die for mine. If I felt I wanted to hurt my children in this way, I would go away as far as possible. When I felt my anger was out of control, that's exactly what I did. I never beat or physically hurt my children, although they got a tap on the nappy when they misbehaved, I generally called a conference and I would explain why they could not do or behave in a certain way, when I called conference they knew they had stepped over a line, I have always been there to support them and help them, I always will be. My Son and daughter are proud and secure, they love, they have true hearts and I am so proud of them, they are very special, and I told them every day how much I loved them. For me a father's love is every bit as important as a mother's love, and men should never be afraid to express this. I can remember one night when I was about four or five years old, I can see it in my mind's eye now! I went to kiss my dad goodnight, he stopped me and said, "Boys don't kiss their fathers. men shake hands." So he shook my hand, I remember feeling so sad when I went to bed that night and I never forgot it. Every day I kiss my son, he is thirty three years of age, and is six foot five inches tall, and he hugs me, he says I am the best dad in the world and is very proud of me. This is my son, the most beautiful gift a father could want. My beautiful Daughter is equal. I can't understand my father. Call it fear or conditioning, call it what you want, but at the end of the day, we all have to live with ourselves. My father is dead now, he had a heart attack and was gone in seconds, my mother and I had not spoken for many years. Sometimes I think this is sad, but because I know the truth, it's better if I am far away from it all. then the secrets, stay secret. There is no healing in secrets!!! My brothers and sisters did not escape my father's wrath, not so long ago they blamed me for what he did. It's ironic, they spoke with my mother and father, but they didn't speak with me. Our parents had so much control over them and they were blind to the manipulation. I married young, I was twenty years old, I had to get away. I had far too many confrontations with my father as I grew up, my mother made me promise not to hit my father, and it's a promise I have kept. this was the promise my mother kept me too. When my father beat me as a teenager and young adult I took it, and when he beat my mother I stepped in and took the beating for her. My father wanted to prove he was the best, and for my mother he was. I can never remember my mother protecting me, but I do remember saying, "One day I would kill my father" One night I waited for him to sleep, I had a knife beside my bed, when he slept I was going to kill him, I was twelve years old. I was going to stab him and cut his heart out, But I fell asleep before he did, because he was working late as a truck driver, and it was late when he came home and went to sleep. My mother found the knife the next morning, as I was getting ready for school, my mother asked me what was I going to do with the knife, I told her and she made me promise that I was never to do that, and that I would never lay a hand on my father, she said I would have been put away in a boys prison, I said I didn't care because they would be safe from my father, but as usual I did what she asked. My brother and sister said I did not protect them, they said I left them alone with my father, and he could concentrate on them. In reality this man tried to intimidate me even when I was married. But now I had my own home, and I could close the door. My father never told me I was good at anything, It didn't matter how good I was, I was never good enough.

CHAPTER EIGHT

When you do not respect yourself, you do not respect anyone or anything else. Life is a precious gift, and I believe we return to spirit after we die. Life goes on when we die, we are mourned or we mourn the loss of a loved one or friend, we are only here for a short time, yet we are so hurtful to each other, we try to prove we are better than ! instead of equal too ! so in so many cases people undermine others to make themselves look or feel better, we should treat people and our loved ones as we wish to be treated, there is not one of us who is perfect, we are products of our life lessons, but we can change our belief systems, and because my father was an asshole does not mean I have to continue the cycle, I am the power in my life, it is my decision what and how I behave, so why can't we respect that life is about learning and we should take the good and go forward with that, be kind to ourselves and every thing and person around us. When we destroy the life of a person, tree, plant or animal, we destroy a part of ourselves. We are all connected and part of a much bigger picture. It is not necessary to kill or fight what we do not understand, all we need is to respect that it is different, then we can study and try to learn to understand. One time I tried to take the life of another man, I was working and we had a confrontation, I told him not to start with me, he did not respect the fact that it was possible I could cause him so much harm. I offered him a way out of the confrontation, but because he thought he was a great boxer, he threw the first punch. He connected very well, and nearly knocked me out, my legs were gone and my body felt weird, I just wanted to lie down, but then my instincts kicked in, he came in to finish the job, and what a surprise he got, I am strong and I stayed on my feet, and then I began to fight back and I tried to take his life away. I did not have a weapon; I used my instincts and physical power. The man very nearly died. It took five people to stop me from choking him to death, and three people to revive him. As I looked at this person unconscious on the ground, I wanted him dead. The rage inside was consuming me, the rage needed respect and control, or someone was going to die, now I was ready to kill, and in the days after, I began to understand this. I have no fear of any man, and I am prepared to die in the protection of my family. If this man had hurt me, my family would have suffered. In my life now, I do respect this rage and I do control it. But when it is very strong, and I feel it rising, I have to go to the gym. This is where I release my rage, I work my ass off and push until I'm tired. Respecting life and people is very important. we need to respect ourselves and who we are, inside is a primal instinct for survival. Because I know there are people who have had similar experiences, I hope they will find some peace and understanding here, I understand what it is like to feel total despair, feeling alone, and no one to talk to. it can feel like you are losing your sanity and total belief in yourself. Nowhere to turn, and afraid to ask for help, worried about what others may think. Abuse comes in many forms, and it's terrifying when you feel so alone. But when you begin to abuse yourself, you need to look inside, you need to accept that you are in trouble and look for help. Find your spirit and slowly teach yourself that you are in control of all things pertaining to yourself, you are the boss of you. In any relationship you only have fifty percent control of that relationship, you can only control yourself, but you are responsible one hundred percent for your actions. You are important no matter what anyone says, you are valuable, So Believing in yourself is the first step to connecting with your spirit, try to believe you are special. I am certain there are many people, who think this life is hard and nobody cares, well let me say this, it takes courage to look at your life, and admit that you have made mistakes. Your life is in your control. How you think and what you want is the way it will be for you. Is it not better to be loving, productive, happy, kind, helpful? If you create this, it will come to you. Your mind creates your reality. it's all about perspective, So start to believe life is beautiful, and someone does care, but start caring for yourself, create the beauty in your life. I had many experiences in my life, some good and some not so good. I was told I was nothing important, But even as a child I was spiritual, I could see things and beings, my mother told me it was the devil and I should stop, or he would come for me, my grandmother told me I was special, and she was always right. I believed in my Grandmother, she was so kind and gentle, and I loved her so much, and now I believe in me because she taught me to. My Grandmother is an angel who watches over me, I should be dead but at the last second she saves me, and we still speak now, she is always beside me. I just wish she was still here in life.

CHAPTER NINE

Now let's talk about fear and what it can do to you. Fear is like a cancer, it grows inside and eventually takes over your life, it takes your life away from you. There are many situations of fear, but there is only one real fear, the fear that you are not strong enough to believe in yourself. I have made fear my friend, I understand it and embrace it. I know fear is an emotion, and like all emotions, we can control them. The fear makes us think "I can't do it," What if." The fear of pain, of being alone, of what someone might say, the fear of failure, the fear of. losing, the fear of evil, and my greatest fear, was the fear of the dark and what it brings. The fear of the dark has a strong bearing on what I am going to say, because I believed this was the time when the devil or evil spirit came for me. I was totally terrified of the dark as a child. Because this is when they came. My father knew we were afraid and when we went to bed, if we spoke to each other, he would turn out the lights. I would try and ease the fear in my brothers and sisters, even though I was terrified, I would say, "Don't worry, it's okay." I would sing to them as quietly as I could, so they would be okay. Or I would tell them nice stories and just talk to them so they would not be afraid. When my father heard us, he would come into our rooms, slap us, and drag us out of bed, we were brought out to the back garden, and put in the coal shed, but this place was cold and dirty, and the dog slept there. it was full of spiders, and creepy crawlies. We were wearing our pyjama's, and had no shoes, we would be in there for God knows how long. I never remember being brought back into the house, or being washed, the place was filthy dirty, and it was totally black, cold and dark. Our feet were so cold, and were black from the coal in the shed, but our bed clothes were always clean. My father always made sure we were terrified. On occasion he would keep one of us in the house with him. My mother worked some evenings, and or late nights, and when my father was sleeping she would bring us into the house, I assume she would wash us, but when you are terrified your mind sometimes forgets for your protection. My mother was also afraid of my father, so the abuse continued, we suffered a lot at the hands of my father. We were always afraid, terrified of the next moment, not knowing what was going to happen, but as I said this was normal for us. When the night came and my father thought we were asleep, he would turn off the lights, this was when I was most terrified, and it was in this time they would come. As I would sleep, I would feel the pressure on my bed, then they would hold me down, I couldn't see what it was, but the pressure on my body was tremendous. I could not move or breathe, I was suffocating, it pushed my face into the pillow, I couldn't turn my head, I wanted to call my mother for help, but I couldn't make a sound, I thought my neck was going to break, I was screaming in my mind. I didn't make any noise, my body hurt, this thing was having sex with me. I wasn't big enough or strong enough to get it off me, I couldn't move, paralysed with fear, my mind just couldn't cope, I could feel its breath on the back of my neck as it held me down, and its weight on my body, It seemed to last forever. I prayed to Jesus, and his mother to help me, I asked God to protect me, when the pressure stopped, I was too frightened to move, or open my eyes or speak in case this thing was still in my room. I never spoke about this in case it was the devil, and he would come back for me. I remember I always thought if I said anything, people would think I was mad, so I said nothing. If I didn't speak, it would go away. The problem was, it didn't go away, and every so often it would return, with the same devastating results.

I never spoke about this for many years. One day I told my mother, she said I was dreaming. It was some dream, because my body hurt for days. So, you see, fear can do many things, even make you question your sanity. My mother also called me a liar.

When I was having my nervous breakdown, or at least I think that was what I was having, the fear I had was so great, I was afraid my children would experience what I did and the devil would come for them. I would sit with them all night and watch them, I slept only for a couple of hours every night, when daylight broke, I knew they were safe because it would not come in the daylight. I only trusted my wife with our children, I worked all day in a very stressful job, and many times I would fight someone, sometimes more than one person, but I had no fear of pain. The pain I liked!!! No matter what was in front of me, if I could hit it, I had no fear of it. To this day I have no fear of any man. When the night came, I needed to protect my children. My beautiful wife tried to help me, but I didn't need, want or accept help, I needed nothing and no one. I was going totally crazy. This went on for nine months. I was losing everything little by little, I was also losing my sanity. I remembered my experiences with the devil, and my children were not going to have the same experiences. I had my grandmothers rocking chair, so I sat in my Grandmothers rocking chair, rocking back and forth all night, my eyes never leaving my sleeping children. One night I began to speak with my Grandmothers spirit. I felt her presence beside me it was very strong. I could even smell her perfume. I felt her hold my hand, and speak softly to me, like she always did. she began to rub my head, and my right cheek, I always liked when she did that when I was little. She took all my pain away. She said I would be okay, and she said she would protect my children. She told me to sleep, that she would stay with me, she said nothing would happen to my babies. I was to rest and get better. That night I cried for hours, and I said to the devil, "If you want my children, you will need to go through me, or take me first!" When morning came, my children were okay, and that was when I started to get better. I have no fear of anything now, but I respect what fear is, I can use fear and control fear when I need to. I thank the spirit that is my Grandmother she is always there for me.

Soon after this I started to look in to spirituality, I truly believe, that in the times when my life was tested, my Grandmother protected me, without her I believe I would be dead, she taught me to believe in myself, and she is always with me. I speak of this because even on my darkest day, when I felt I was losing my sanity, and everything seemed over for me, and I wanted to die she was there for me. There is always hope, this hope can come in the form of a person, or a thing, or in my case, a beautiful spirit. To my Grandmother, I love you, your grandchildren and great great grandchildren are healthy and happy, and I know you protect them for me. The spirit lives on in the love you share with someone, my love for my grandmother is infinite. I feel it every day, and it never changes for me, I love her as much now as I ever did. So you see, fear is only an emotion, and it can be controlled. But love is spirit, that needs to be expressed. In my life I have had many lessons, and I feel that love is the best lesson I have learnt. As my life takes its course, there will be many challenges. But I am sure, what I have learnt and experienced, will help me face it bravely. Please remember always, you are in this life to express. So choose your experiences with care, It is not important what has happened before, you cannot change that, but you have the power to change what you take from your experiences now, so choose the best for you.

Insecurity is also an emotion, so don't make it a state of mind, or a way of life. Many times, I have experienced insecurity, and it's amazing what we believe when we have insecurities and we don't fully believe in ourselves. This is a lesson my father taught me. I cannot remember as a child or a young man, anytime when my father said I did well, nor did he ever say "Well done son." He was always the best, and anything I did was never good enough. So I spent most of my life looking for his praise, chasing his affection and approval, When I was about nineteen years old, I gave my mother more money than my father earned every week, I worked hard, and I was the best butcher I could be, my father was always jealous of my relationship with my mother. I worshipped my mother, and if I had an argument with her, in the morning or afternoon, she had flowers or chocolate, in the evening, to say I am sorry. I always bought her something nice, this drove my father crazy, but we never spoke about it. When I played sport, I was never good enough, and I didn't do this or I didn't do that, I made too many mistakes, I was an idiot, I ran too much, I was a dirty player. I had no skills; I was wasting my time. You know, some of this I believed for a time. And even when people asked me to play football, when they came to my house and offered me money to play or wanted me in fighting competitions. When I did karate, I didn't have the confidence because my father had tutored me all my life and I was scared I would not be good enough I mean my father said I wasn't, so it must have been true. I wanted to be a dancer, my mother wanted me to be an ice skater, but for my father, I was a sissy, and no son of his was going to be a dancer. I loved music, and I could sing. My brothers and sisters always asked me to sing, I used to do impressions, and always made people laugh. I love to play the fool; I suppose because I got a lot of attention. I always did my best in everything I did, and I hoped one day, my Dad would smile and say, "You did good." But you know, I learnt that this wasn't going to happen any day soon. I continued trying, one day I was playing soccer for my team, we had just won the cup, and this game was for the league. It was a tough game and I had given my best all season. I was tired, but I played my heart out.

We played extra time, because I scored the equaliser, I played centre half position. The other team scored again, and then we scored again, and then I scored the winning goal. We won 4-3, my father watched the game, and after he said I was an idiot for running too much, and it was not my job to score goals. We had just won the league, and the cup because I scored the winning goals, and here was my father saying I was no good!!? I was twenty six years old and in fantastic physical condition. I played my heart out, everyone said I was one of the best players they had seen in a long time. I played football six times a week, I went to the gym four times a week, I worked hard to take care of my family, I was honest, and I spoke true. I would help anyone, and my father said I wasn't good enough! we had an argument and he got aggressive, my children were there and I told him not to start anything in front of my children or I would kill him, the lads held both of us back, my wife and children got upset so I told him he was never to come near me or my family again, and it did not matter what he thought of me, In this moment I realized, I could never please him, so I stopped trying. For the next ten years, I never asked him for anything, when he commented on my life, or decisions I made, he was told to mind his own business. From that day, I realised he was a jealous, insecure, twisted person. That year we won the league, the cup, and I was voted player of the year, not for the first time. The sad thing is, that one day my father did say, I was the best player he had ever seen in his life. He said he was very sorry for not helping me, and that he was jealous of my ability. The ironic thing is, his lack of interest in me, made me work harder. When I was younger, I needed him, and he wasn't there for me. I have a son myself, and he is my world, I love him, if he makes mistakes, I will never be disappointed with him. He is a beautiful spirit and I love him dearly, my life is his and his sisters. In a split second I would give my life for either of them, They are my children, and they have my love and protection, Ross and Amy are the reasons I am here. My love for them is complete, the lesson here is to believe in yourself, and be the best you can be. All our lives we are taught conditioning, it comes from our parents, teachers, family and friends. It comes from learning right and wrong, from the people who are supposed to know, and the people we trust. Because these people with the responsibility for teaching us life, and what it is about, what we are supposed to do and how to think. If you don't think and do for yourself, you are being controlled. So when they control us and if we don't do what they say or want, we are punished, and are taught a lesson. So let's look at the lesson, the lesson here is control, they want to control what you think and do. So we trust that they know what is right, we become slaves to a system. But in my experience, all controlling systems are corrupt, because someone else has power over you. The amount of power you give away depends on you. So once again you think you are in control of your life! But we do things to please people, so they won't be angry, or upset. We keep their secrets, so we are good children, friends, workers or partners because maybe have fear of what someone will think of us. So now we are back to conditioning, and control. My point to this is, it is not important what someone else thinks of you. It's only important that you do what is best for you and those around you. Be kind, honest, helpful and loving. It's less stressful to help someone than it is to make problems, take control of and for your actions, and if you can sleep at night and know you have done no harm to anyone, then you have had a good day. Do your best, love and respect yourself, then it is possible you can give your best in every situation. We are all learning in this life, and we sometimes make mistakes.

So control your actions and life, and let everyone else control theirs, you are responsible only for what you say and do. Conditioning is also about control, I was taught to take control of a situation as best I could, I was taught that if someone cries, it's a sign of weakness, that's not true crying is the effect of an emotion. It can be happy, sad, frustration, fear, and many more reasons. But I was taught not to cry, the conditioning here was 'crying was weak. ' I have seen grown men stand stoned faced at their mother's or loved one's funeral, I have seen little boys hold back their tears, when they were hurt, the conditioning that "Boys don't cry! No one will ever see me cry!" It's crap! when you have an emotion it's better to express it, you can cry if you want to. For me when I was younger, I did not cry, and if I made someone cry, I was in control. This is what I was taught. My father would get frustrated because he couldn't make me cry, but he told me crying was weak. He would smack harder to make us cry. He would provoke us and push us until we broke, and we cried with frustration. We did not cry from the pain, only the frustration. When I was young, I promised my brothers and sisters, I would grow up big and strong, and one day I would beat the living daylights out of my father. I began working out when I was seven years old, I did grow up big and strong. I did karate, boxing, weight training and football. I became the best I could be. I was big and nineteen and a half stone with four percent body fat, I was leg pressing six hundred kilo's in the gym, I kept my word, I was aggressive and angry, and I feared no man. Now I was ready, All I needed was an opportunity, but no one wanted me to fight my father, because I would kill him, So again my father was my motivation to be the best I could be. My father taught me so much, and I did the opposite to what he taught me.

CHAPTER TEN

In life we have many experiences, and we may feel that everything is bad, but it is what we take from the experience that is good or bad. My father taught me to be strong, and determined, but he did not intend to do that. He intended to break me, I took the experiences and interpreted them in my own way not in how he taught me. I also learned, that the strength of a man is in his kindness and love, not in his physicality, or ability to knock someone on their ass, any clown can knock someone down, if you can take control of a situation and be in a position of power, it is then you see the measure of a man, real power is in his heart and his intentions. There are many ways of controlling someone, and my father was a monster. As I go through my life, I realise that I am becoming the man I want to be, and it is in spite of my father's teachings, that one good thing I can say he did teach me was, to be a good provider for my family. I also mastered the art of how to manipulate a situation to suit me, I learned that I can control other people, as a younger man I did hurt people, and to all the people in the past to whom I have hurt, I am truly sorry, especially the women. I learnt that it was easy to control people, and I used all kinds of control to get what I wanted. But even a child knows how to control a situation. How many times have you seen a child scream until they get what they want, or cry until you feel sorry for them and you give in. This is all conditioning, we learn from a very young age, when this is how you were taught, it is normal behaviour, when I was very young I took what I wanted, as I grew I asked please, as a young adult I manipulated, and as a man, I used everything in my power and ability, I used my charm, my looks, my body and my sexuality. I learned to pick up on someone's insecurities, manipulate and control them until I got what I wanted. I made love, had sex, and abused women for my pleasure, just because I could. I used sex as a way to control, manipulate, empower myself, and as a weapon. In this too, I was the best I could be. There have been many women in my life, and I even made money from sex. I had affairs with married women, when I lived in America they paid for my apartment and bought me designer clothes, but every women I ever had sex with was a willing entity, I never forced anyone and I loved sex they always left happy, they went back to their families and I never caused anyone of them a problem, we had an agreement and sometimes I made money from it, I know some people will disagree with what I did, but this book is honest and I'm no saint, I was taught that women are weak, and to use them with no respect for them. I did what I wanted, when I wanted. I learned it's very easy to use someone who is insecure, and just as easy if they are strong, everyone has insecurities, we are all controlled by emotion, and if you want, you can control a person totally. With women you cater to their hearts, if you show some compassion and love for them, they are yours and just cater to the male ego and you are sorted. You may not like this but it's true.

When I had my first serious relationship, I thought I was in love with Sarah, she wasn't the first girl I had sex with, but she was my first real love. I remember we had sex everywhere we could. We were always together. I was crazy about her and she was gorgeous too. My father came home one night, and we were lying on my bed, we were not having sex or doing anything other than listening to music, but he went totally crazy. and called me and the girl all the names under the sun. By the way, my father told me nothing about sex, my sister had that privilege, when he found my naked page three girls, and they were only boob/topless pics, he said I was a pervert, and showed my mother, sister, and my girlfriend when we were sitting at the kitchen table one evening, I just wanted to die, I was so embarrassed, He was such a bastard, he would do anything to belittle us. When I began masturbating, I thought that there was something wrong with me. I didn't know what was wrong with me so I never spoke to anyone for years. It wasn't something you spoke about in those days. So the page three girls were innocent enough but he would just be a bastard because he could, later most of the porn I watched was his and it was a lot stronger than page three girls, he was such a hypocrite.

In later years I spoke with my first girlfriend, and she told me that my father had tried to have sex with her shortly after he found us in the bedroom. Our relationship became very intense and it killed the love, I became obsessed that she might cheat or leave me, it was impossible for her to move. I tried to control every move, and after a very bad and tough time, we went our separate ways. But I learned a good lesson in this relationship, I needed to control myself. I met this girl in later years, she got married and had two children, we had an affair for a while, but she got too possessive and demanding, so I walked away. To try to control someone else, or part of their life is no easy task, because you begin to live two lives, yours and theirs. Sometimes you become confused as to who is right and who is wrong, and who's life you are living. I learnt that I was able to do what I wanted, to control the other person, and play around at the same time. After my breakdown and leaving my wife, I didn't trust or believe in anything so I was never faithful or honest, and I played every game I could. I used emotional, sexual insecurities, arrogance, physical, spiritual, any form of manipulation I could, to get what I wanted. I had women coming to me from all directions. I wrecked marriages, relationships, but most of all, lives. I didn't care for anyone or anything. I didn't believe in anything, my marriage broke down, my life was in the toilet. If I could control everyone and everything around me, I would be okay. I had the power to make or break people, and I did. For many years my father would say, if he didn't take care of himself, then who would look after my mother and my sisters and brothers. This made sense to me at that time, so I did look after me. My father was very selfish, and so was I, but even through all of this, I still took care of my wife and children, and in a second I went to them if they had a problem. They were more important to me than I or my life was, I was living my life on a knife edge and any women who I was with always came second to Rie and the kids, I never gave a commitment to anyone, so I lost a great love in my life. Because they could not understand "my children before me" or anyone else. This was part of the reason my second marriage failed, but I have no regrets. When I was twenty, I got married to Rie. The morning of the wedding just before I left the house, my mother stopped me and said I did not have to go through with it. I thought about it for a while and then I said "Rie is waiting." Rie is beautiful, and I would want her in my life even if I had not married her. She is true, honest, a beautiful spirit., and was the best friend I had. The girl did not know what she was getting into with me. Rie came into my life, shortly after my first love Sarah and I broke up, Rie and I became good friends, and I trusted her completely, we were in love. About two years into our relationship, she met a man, and became friends with him they both worked at nursing, she said they were just friends, he used to buy her flowers n gifts and she accepted them, I had quietened down and I accepted her reasons but it hurt a little, we were planning to get married, so I was a little annoyed and jealous, we had a fight and I told her she had to choose, she chose me. Six months later we got married, and this man came to the wedding, we had another fight on our wedding day.

As time went by, I tried to forget, but I felt a little betrayed, and insecure. Rie was everything to me, and she had everything I could give her. A beautiful home, and a very good lifestyle. We were relatively happy, and we didn't argue much. I think we had three serious arguments in seven years, but something inside me never forgot what happened, just before she told me she was pregnant, I had thought about finishing our relationship, but when she was pregnant I was so excited, I always wanted a baby. I wanted a son, and I was sure I had one, I awaited my child, and took extra care of Marie, she did not have to do anything. I spoke every day with my son as he grew inside her. The day my son was born, it rained cats and dogs. Thunder rocked the sky and the lightning lit up the stars. But for me I had my boy, he was beautiful, and from that moment we have been together. Now I had my family, the most important thing in my world. About a year before this, my father had a massive heart attack, I waited in work and he never came to collect me, I called my sister and she told me what had happened, but I felt there was something really wrong. I went to the hospital to see him; my brother came too. When I saw my dad, I was heartbroken, the man I remember as a child, always big and strong, afraid of nothing, he was my dad, the best in the world. Even though he treated us like dogs, he was my dad. He lay in the bed, with tubes sticking out of him, connected to machines. He looked at my brother and said, "I am Sorry for what I did to you, I love you son, you take care of yourself." He looked at me, and I wanted him to say he loved me too, but he said, "I'm dying, take care of your mother and the family." I said they are not my responsibility, so he had to get better and look after my mother and family himself, and he did get better. The day Rie said she was pregnant, my father was by my side, I was taught to take care of my family from an early age, and I continue to do so. I am not as close to them as I used to be, but when there is a problem, they call me. Rie and I were very happy, and the next year, we had another beautiful child, a little girl Amy. The most special and beautiful gift I could have asked for, now my family was complete. Now it was two years since my father's heart attack, I had a beautiful family, I was content. Rie and I were good, my father and I had a better relationship, to a degree. But something was wrong, I could feel it, and I knew something big was coming. My wife and the children were fine, we had everything. I didn't know at the time that my relationship with my children was different. With my son I was at ease, but with my daughter I was afraid of her, I knew I loved them both, but I couldn't understand why I was feeling so afraid, she was my little girl, and I had a fear of being close to her when she was naked, with my son I had no problem. When my daughter was dressed, I would play with her and loved her. but with Ross I did everything, I just couldn't understand my fear of Amy One day I spoke with my cousin, who I had been very close too, all my teenage years, and she was a spiritual person, she spoke of her life and her problems, and I spoke of mine. I expressed my fear, and she told me why she turned to drugs. When she was little she was sexually abused by an aunt and uncle of ours. She was only little at the time; she did speak to her mother and father about it but was told not to be telling lies. This went on for some time, I spent many years with these people too and I knew the violence of my uncle. When I was four or five years old, he beat me very badly, because I was crying for my grandmother. She had gone to the shops, and I woke him up when I was calling for her. He threw me across the room, I hit the wall and then fell on the sofa, and then onto the floor. This man was a total aggressive bastard, when I lived with my grandmother my aunt used to come to my room when I was in bed, I thought I was only dreaming for years, when she used to touch me. But even as an adult, my dreams of her were always sexual. in the dreams my body wasn't developed, I had the body of a little boy. As a young teenager, she used to show us her breasts. she would perform oral sex on me sometimes. I spoke to my brother one time, and he said she did the same to him. I was beginning to understand my fear of my daughter, but inside I knew she was my baby girl, and I would never touch her. My fear was that someone would say I was a pervert. The fear separated me from my daughter, from having a normal relationship, and being comfortable with my child. Everything started to come together for me in my mind, I started to remember times, places, and people. I had one question still unanswered.

My sisters were in contact with these people too, I looked at my two sister's behaviour over the years, and I concluded that they had been abused, it nearly killed me. All my life I thought I had protected them, for me something broke inside. I asked my mother if it was true, and she said, "No!" She said my cousin was putting ideas in my head and she was a liar, my mother always protected my father and her family, she did nothing for us, her children. I never spoke about me or the abuse that happened to me. For me I could take it, but for my sisters I was devastated. I told my mother, if she had lied to me, I would never speak to her again. For me! life was normal even with all the violence, well I thought it was normal. I channelled all my aggression into any sport I was doing at the time. So my wife and children were never afraid, or hurt by me. They had my love, and protection, and no reason to fear me whatsoever. Rie tried to speak to me about my relationship with our daughter, why was I a little different with her than I was with our son, but I wasn't able to explain. once my daughter was dressed, I treated her the exact same as my son. I loved her with all my heart. I also spoke to my mother about my fear, and she said I was being stupid, but for me it was a very real fear. To this point I was the ideal husband, father, and son. but I was starting to crack, I was losing control of myself. I walked out of my job, I was totally angry, I was falling apart. I went to my cousin again, and I asked her if she knew anything about my sisters. She told me to speak with my sisters. as she could not say, as it wasn't her place. Now I was sure, because she always spoke the truth, and now she was avoiding answering me. I left her home and drove to my sister's house. She was surprised when I asked my question. At first she said "No!", but when I said I would get an answer from my uncle, she burst into tears, I nearly fell through the floor, I wanted to kill him, but first I needed to help my sister. She asked me not to do anything, because she had her family, her children and husband. she would die of embarrassment. When I looked at her, I saw my little sister, A blonde, blue eyes innocent child. Always smiling at her big brother, believing he would protect her from all the bad things in life, and I tried. I put my arms around her, and said I would protect her, and her secret. It was killing me, and now for my second question, my younger sister? I remember the same answer. I just burst into tears, now everything I had feared had come true. My younger sister was always following me around, when she was little. She was like a little puppy. She had big beautiful eyes and dark curly hair. She loved me dearly, as I did her. Sometimes she made me crazy, but I loved her with all of my heart. Now I understand why they came into my bed, for protection, truly believing I could help them, I always thought I did protect them, but I was wrong. My third question was even more devastating, I asked how old they were, when it began. My sister said, about three years of age. Something inside me snapped, I just broke inside, I wanted to be sick, my head was spinning, I began to shake, and a rage was so powerful I wanted to explode. Now I was going to prison!!! because I was going to kill this man and his sister, my aunt and uncle. But first I had to deal with my mother. I asked if my father knew, my sister said no, but our mother knew. I had to control myself, I made some tea, spoke a little more to my sister, and promised not to do, or say anything, she was so upset. I made a promise, and to this day I never spoke to this man again. It's ironic, he had both legs amputated, so now he understands what it is like to be helpless and have someone else controlling your life. His sister died in her own vomit, after a heavy drinking session. She was alone.

Before I left my sister, she told me that it was my father that had abused her and my younger sister. Something inside me broke, my heart snapped I was devasted, but I had to keep my promise not to say anything, everything I believed in died that day. Now for my mother! When I left my sisters, I went to my mothers, she was cooking dinner for my brothers and my father, my brothers still lived at home. One was about twenty and the other one was only fourteen years old. My mother knew I was coming, as my sister had called her to tell her. When I arrived, my mother was as white as a ghost, I didn't have to say a word, she said "Now calm down, it's okay, everything will be okay, you need to remember, if anyone finds out, your sisters will be hurt, say nothing to no one, not even your father, and your brothers must never find out, it will kill them, they are not strong like you!" I stood there, and I didn't even blink. I asked how long she knew, and she said shortly after it began. I asked her what did she do, she said she stopped it. I asked her about both my sisters, she said she did not know about my youngest sister, until after she got married. She was having problems and spoke to my older sister, who in turn spoke to my mother. I told my mother she was a liar, and to never speak to me again, that all the family values she taught me were bullshit, and for me I did not believe in family. I walked out and went home. I didn't speak to Marie about this for many years, I was just so upset. A little time after this I fell apart and the dreams began, and I thought the devil was going to take my children. My sisters went to a counsellor with my mother, but as usual, my mother picked the wrong one, they asked me to come with them one day to help them, I went and I listened to them speak. I just wanted to die, they spoke about what had been done to them, the counsellor looked at me and asked why I was so angry. He said I had no right to be so angry, it didn't happen to me. Little did he know. I asked him, was he ever in my position. He answered, "No!" I told him not to tell me how I should be feeling, and if he spoke another word, I would throw him out of the window. We were on the third floor! Then I left, for me, things got progressively worse, I got more and more violent, I took a job as a bouncer, and security guard, in one of the toughest areas in Dublin, I fought every day, sometimes two and three times a day. I liked to hit people, and I hit many, I gave no ground, and asked for none. I did this job for two years; my marriage broke down. I was afraid I would hurt my wife and my children. So I left, I had an affair and went away. My son spoke to me on the phone and I returned to my home, Rie let me stay, and I watched my children every night in case the devil came. I was having a nervous breakdown, Rie did not know how to help me, my family did nothing to help, Shortly after I got better, I left again, I believed my wife deserved so much better, I didn't trust anyone, and my wife could not get close to me, My wife gave her best and all she got back was pain. I took care of my family, and my wife agreed she would stop work and take care of the children, and I would take care of everything else. We did this for about ten years. Shortly before I left my wife, I became a gym instructor, teaching aerobics, when I nearly killed that man, I knew I had to change my life, so I began to study spirituality and began using my energy in a more positive, constructive way. I studied hard and became the best trainer I could be, I was very spiritual and became very quiet and peaceful, my life was getting better. I apologised to my wife for all the hurt I caused her and explained what had happened or some of what happened, I loved her and the children, we agreed to stay friends, and we have been close friends ever since. She is truly an angel. My wife will always have a place in my heart. In my spirituality, I became more aware of my abilities, I learned a lot of different things, but one of the strongest was, my ability to know and see things, I worked with energy healing, and I was remembering lots of things from my past. It was in this time I met Tina, I studied hard to be a good trainer, and also practised staying calm through my spiritual learning, I had learned to channel spirit, heal the emotions, and spirit in people, I learned to teach and live in a more spiritual way, and I worked with a lot of people, my healing was done with love, compassion and understanding I did the best I could, I was able to see and feel a person's pain, but most of all, my connection to my family got stronger, I knew when they were having problems and what the problems were, and I helped them as much as I could, the rage inside me was quiet, and certainly under control. I had one or two short term relationships, but it was mainly for sex, and my mind accepted them as learning experiences. I was becoming a different man, able to forgive and cope with all my experiences, I had learned so much, and accepted I could not change the past, but had to live with it and I tried my best. I meditated twice a day, and everything was quiet within me.

Now I was ready to give and receive love. I was in perfect physical condition, bronzed, strong, muscular and boy I looked good! My spirit was quiet, I was confident, and ready to take on the world. All my ghosts were sleeping, when in walked Tina, the attraction was purely sexual, you could cut the energy with a knife. We met, it was lust, at first sight. We made love for hours, and our relationship began. Tina was beautiful, and I fell in love with her, she became one of the most important people in my life. We were together every moment we could, be. Most of the time in bed, she had a free spirit, and I really loved her, I trusted her completely, and I would always be faithful to her. She understood my children came first, and everything was great. We had our problems, not least from her family, I was a warlock and Tina was under my spell, or so her mother said, a more idiotic woman I have never met.

I practised Shamanism, the native American way, because I felt a strong desire and understanding with them. I had done past life regression, and in four lifetimes, I was a Native American, so this was the path I chose to walk. I was peaceful and quiet, I respected everyone, and everything. I made no problems for anyone, I gave my best to Rie and the children, and to Tina, but to Tina's mother, I was an evil warlock trying to possess her daughter, because I had an altar with stuff for doing evil magic, in fact I had a table with crystals and sage on it. Tina's mother offered me 10,000 euro to leave her daughter. She went to my family, told lies to Tina, and anyone who would listen. The night she offered me the money, she told Tina I was with another woman, that she saw me in a car at the garage. The woman I was with, was her! and she asked me not to say anything to Tina. So when Tina asked me where I was, I lied. Tina checked and knew I was lying, I told Tina what happened. her mother denied it, and we had a big argument. Eventually I went to the house and confronted Tina's mother.

She then told the truth, but not before she caused so much trouble, according to her mother, I was beating Tina, and she was afraid so this was her reason for causing so much trouble, Tina and I had moved in together about six months before this all began, I never went near her mother's house for a long time. Through all of this I stayed quiet, I was in love with Tina and I wasn't going to lose her. I grew stronger in my spiritual learning and was able to see problems before they came. I could feel them. One day when Tina and I had gone away for a weekend, I was sitting on a cliff beside the ocean, and I saw a young woman's face in the water, I wasn't sure who the woman was for a while but then realised it was my grandmother, I then felt my family, and a huge sadness within, I spoke to Tina and said we had to go home, She said I was crazy, and we should phone first. I said "no!" She could come or stay, but I had to go. It was nearly 500 miles, as I drove, I felt everything, and I was near tears, I knew someone had died and I knew it was a child. As I got close, I knew it was my brother's child, I went to my house and tried to call my sister, but got no answer, so I went straight to the hospital. When I walked in, everyone looked at me, and asked what I was doing there, how did I know where to go? I hadn't spoken to anyone and everybody was in tears, my youngest brother had his baby girl in his arms, he asked me to take her and make her better, I looked at him, he was heartbroken. He asked me to please help him, but I could only look at him, I couldn't even speak, he asked because I was spiritual, and he believed I could make his little girl live. I stood there, totally helpless, my whole family looked at me in expectation, I could do nothing.

The next few days were very hard for my family, and when my little niece was being buried, I did not go, because my mother said, I couldn't bring Tina, and Rie together, she was worried about what people might say. After this, I stopped meditating and my spiritual work went also, I never wanted to know if my family were in trouble again, not in this way. I had dealt with many things good and bad, but this was really bad for me. I stayed faithful to Tina for three years, on her birthday she was twenty nine, She said she was going to meet her family for a drink, and she would return home about 9:00PM, I said I would make dinner, I had a present and flowers for her, I waited all night and she never came home, about 3:00AM. I was so angry, I went to look for her, I found her in the arms of another man, kissing him outside a disco, the same place I had taken her many times. I wanted to kill her, we had a big row, and I threw her out, now everything changed in me again, I became a complete bastard, six months later I took Tina back, but I cheated on her with everyone I could, I used and abused. I made as many problems as I could, but the best was yet to come, I knew that Tina's family business revolved around her, so now I was going to take her to America away from her family, this created lots of problems, the relationship was absolutely crap, but I was determined to cause problems, after two more years in Ireland, and a new home we bought together, new cars, and with her family business thriving, and after many affairs, I asked her to come to America with me, I convinced her it was for the best. So we made the decision to go. Now I really got them, I taught them a good lesson, but I forgot I had to leave my children in the rage, which lasted three years. I did not think I would have to leave my children, but it was too late, I never realised that hurting Tina and her family would also hurt my children and Rie.

We went to America and I soon developed relationships with other women, I was so angry, I was going to make problems for everyone. I had Five affairs in six months, Tina suspected, but she could not prove anything. Then I met my future second wife, I began a relationship with this girl, and I played one woman off the other. One day Tina said something about my children and that was it, now it was over. I moved out and into my own apartment, I had a relationship with Eri. One night Tina got very drunk and not for the first time, she called me at 4:00AM, she was very upset, I knew she was in trouble, I went to see her, she had vomited everywhere, it was in her hair, on the bed, on the floor, in the sink on top of the dishes, The apartment was in chaos, I took her out of bed and put her in a chair, Then I changed the bed, I got in the shower with her and washed her as she couldn't stand up. I dried her and put her into bed. I cleaned the apartment and did the laundry, she asked me to stay, by now it was 7:00AM, later that morning I called her father in Ireland and spoke with him, He asked me why I beat Tina, plus a lot of other stuff, I explained the situation, and told him I would call him later. Tina asked me to stay with her, so I sat in the chair, when she woke up we talked, and I told her she had to speak with her father and tell him the truth, she wanted me to come back so She told the truth I think for the first time in her life. She was very violent when she drank too much, She got hurt with me because she would fight me in a rage, I would not let her hurt me, and I defended myself by blocking the kicks and punches and restraining her, One time she put me out of work for months when she kicked me in the knee, so yes she got hurt, because I was very strong, but the girl had courage or she was stupid. When everything settled, her father apologised to me, and thanked me for taking care of Tina. within a couple of weeks Tina returned home, but she came back to the USA, and Soon after she closed my bank account, and took all the money out, she went on a holiday to the Caribbean with her boyfriend, who she was seeing when she was still with me. and spent my money, god she had some balls. She married this man and they have two children last I heard. By the way she never returned the money. When I was in America, I was dating a beautiful South American girl she was so pretty, with an accent to die for. when she spoke to me, I melted. She was crazy about me, and I about her. But all my hurt and conditioning kicked in, also my relationship with Tina was not long finished, so I was not in a good place, remember I was taught to trust no one, and always get them before they get me, my parents were great teachers. I was working as a personal trainer, gym instructor. I was a handsome guy with great body and an Irish brogue, the women loved me, and I loved them back, I had stopped my spiritual work a few years now, I believed in nothing and I was a complete arsehole, so the poor girl didn't know what hit her, she had a kind heart and loving soul. So we decided to move in together. I had been living on my own for about a year and had been sleeping with women for money. I had five ladies I was having affairs with, and each one paid for services and my beautiful girlfriend had not a clue. I got into construction, and had my own company, I had seven guys working for me, we made a fortune. I travelled home to Ireland four times a year and stayed with my ex wife and children. I bought suitcases full of presents home for all my family, brothers, sisters, nieces, nephews, my kids and ex wife, also my mother and father. I worked hard and I played hard. I loved my girlfriend very much, but my issue with trust were huge. I trusted nobody. I took care of her and we travelled lots, we had lots of money, cars, and a lovely home. I had it all. Once again, I began my life with Eri, she was my friend in need. She was from Chile, in South America, but had lived in the US for eighteen years, she was very pretty, and had a good sweet spirit, but she could not calm me. When I finished with Tina, I had gone so far back. I trusted no one, I cheated, I lied, I played with people's lives. I had no strength or confidence, so I made everyone pay, especially Eri. She was my next victim. She made it very easy, because she was so innocent, Eri was a beautiful woman, with beautiful eyes, and a smile that could stop traffic, also she touched my heart with her kindness and compassion. I would like to thank you, and if you ever read this book, I hope you understand, I wasn't angry with you. I was angry at the world. You have my deepest respect, and I apologise from my heart for any wrong I have done to you. Eri paid for all the wrongs in my life. In many ways, she reminded me of my mother, and I realised I wanted to hurt my mother not Eri. She gave her best but wasn't strong enough to be with me. I would have destroyed her personally, she gave seven years of her life to me, and a lot of herself to help me. When times were good, they were very good. But when it was bad, we didn't even communicate, for me her weakness was that she would speak to anyone who would listen, and never accept she was responsible for herself, or any part of what was happening, just like my mother, I loved Eri very much, but she was looking for the perfect man, or at least her interpretation of who he was, and believe me, I could never be that man. She would tell me the man of her dreams; it is quite possible I was her worst nightmare. It's funny how they say, you look for a partner like your mother or father. For me, she had a lot of my mother's traits, and for her, my anger represented her father. As I tried to explain, I was a man who had a lot of emotions, and sometimes I expressed anger, but unlike her father or my father and mother, I was never physically violent with her. one day we had a blazing row and I was so angry, I had found a bank book in her name that she never told me about, I always put my money on the table, she knew what I earned every week, but she hid the book, I was furious and said I was going to kill her, she stood looking at me and said go ahead hit me, so I hit the wall putting my fist through a glass picture and shredding my hand with the glass, there was blood everywhere, she then said sit down babe and let me clean your hand up, she did not fear me for sure, she knew I would never touch her in a violent way. I was angry sometimes, but I also knew how to love, when you are in a situation where you have another person involved, you can only control 50% of the situation, because you can only be responsible for your own actions. As a man I am totally responsible for what I say and do, I began walking my spiritual path, a long time ago, and I have been on and off of it many times, I believe it's your interpretation that makes a situation either joyous or bad. Sometimes people get hurt, if your intention is on this purpose, then you really need to ask yourself why. Some people say, he/she made me do it. But in truth, the last thought or decision, is with you. You decide what you want to do. You are totally responsible for your actions. It's funny, my mother blames everything on my father, and on everyone else. My father blamed my mother, his father and everyone else. My brothers and sisters blamed everyone because they have problems. It seems everyone blames everyone else. I think it's time to stop making excuses for our behaviour and start taking responsibility for our actions and ourselves.

CHAPTER ELEVEN

Every Christmas Eri went home to Chile, and I went home to Ireland. Then I would meet her in Chile and spend a few weeks there on holiday. Life was great and the money was rolling in. One day I got a call from my mother, saying my father would like to visit so I sent them tickets. They came for a week to visit me in New York, what a nightmare. My father caused a lot of issues, this was the first time my girlfriend had met them, and they stayed with us. My mother loved my girlfriend, but my father not so much. She was gorgeous, but again, my father disapproved. The trip ended with bad feeling. They went home much too my relief, I looked at them differently, knowing what I knew. but a part of me craved my father's affection and approval. As I said, I was making huge money, and a little while later my mother called and said they were struggling, I said I would send them some money, but my father said he would rather come and work for it.

So I sent a ticket and he came over. My girlfriend and he bounced off each other, I was so stressed out I was paying him 1500 dollars a week. After a month of total stress, he said he was going home. My girlfriend was going to leave me, he turned my life upside down. It turned out that he had walked into the bathroom while she was in the shower, and he tried it on with her. He would not leave the bathroom so she said she was going to tell me, now he had really fucked up, and he was going home, but she never told me about that incident until many years later. So once again, my father couldn't behave himself. He begrudged me any happiness and he always found a way to belittle and upset me. No matter what or how good I was. A few years later, my son who was fourteen years old, and when I was home for Christmas and he asked me to come home for good. So within four weeks I was home, I gave the business to the lads, and my girlfriend stayed and sold everything, then she followed me to Ireland. A little time later we got married, everything was so much harder for us in Ireland, I was working sixteen hours a day, when I came in from work she was going out to work, a year later we lost our baby, and my wife went back to Chile. After about a year I tried to work things out with Eri but she would not come back to Ireland, So I did what I always did, I walked away from her, and I had affairs, I never had much trouble getting women, but as soon as someone said, "I love you," it triggered something in me, my mind said I am not loveable, how could you love me? when the people who were supposed to love me, betrayed me so badly? so again the cycle started. When I lived in the states, I spent time with Native Americans, I had done ceremonies with them, and was looking into their way of life, traditions and customs. Just for a little while I found peace, but any connection or contact with my parents, pulled me out of my place of peace. Back in Ireland things were tough, I was driving a taxi for a while, which gave me the opportunity to meet plenty of women. So being single again, I took full advantage of it. One day a guy I was training in the gym, asked if I was interested in bouncing work, door security. I said yes if the money was good, I had plenty of experience. I worked on doors for many years. So the cycle of violence began again. The guy told me the place I would be working was a piece of cake, easy money a retirement home lol. My God, it was a tough door! I earned my stripes there, I had a great reputation, and lots of people knew me. I could negotiate and calm situations down, I was a talker, so I generally resolved conflicts, but when I had to throw down, I did it with no hesitation. I could always fight. I always tried to be fair, and let the idiot walk away, but when it kicked off, I always kept control of myself, because I hit very hard and I feared I might kill someone with a punch. When the guy was under control I would stop and give the guy an opportunity to go home. I never hurt anyone just because I could. But no matter who came at me, I would never be intimidated. This was the first place I had a hit put on me and I had a confrontation with one of the top drug dealers around, he said I would be dead by the end of the week, I called some people I know and they sorted it for me. As a child, my father would push and push, poking me and trying to intimidate me, trying to provoke a reaction, where I would hit out. I would hold my temper and frustration, because I would get the shit beaten out of me if I struck out at him. In effect, he taught me control. I learned my lesson well, I understood the difference between reaction and response, a reaction being something that happens in the moment, it's instinct, a response takes a few seconds longer, I was never a hard man or arrogant, when I was in these situations, as the person standing in front of me, had a fifty-fifty chance. I didn't know who he was, or if he was good or even better than me, so I never knew if I was going to get hurt or not. But I always made sure I was the last one standing. I did this work for many years, and made plenty of enemies, I even had two hits put on my life by drug dealers. There were very few nights I didn't fight. I have been injured many times, but I never lost a fight. Every idiot I hit was a bully just like my father. I made a lot of money doing that work, and I made some lifelong friends. I was good at what I did, I never backed down when it came to it, and I wasn't shy about throwing a punch. So once again, my life was full of violence. I couldn't go anywhere without wondering if someone would see me and remember me from some incident on a door. When I was out dating I would sit with my back to a wall and face the door so I could see who came in, I would sit at the back of a cinema so nobody could sit behind me, and I was always on my guard, just in case. Sure enough it did happen many times, I had many confrontations when I was out with my family and friends, I had the respect of my work mates and the Gardai, I was well known and worked on some of the toughest doors in the Country. The best compliment I ever received was from my friends wife, it was the first time we met in person and it was at John's 40th birthday party, she came and kissed me on the cheek and gave me a hug, she said to me that she knew her husband was always safe when he worked with me, I said thank you, but it's the other way around, as he kept me safe. Myself and John are still friends today and I love this guy!! We stood shoulder to shoulder many times, and I always knew I was safe. We had knives and guns pulled on us and we were outnumbered many times, we stood our ground, and he always backed me up, we also had great laughs, he could tell a great story. he is a gentleman and has my total respect.

CHAPTER TWELVE

For many years now, I have known the truth about my family, I never spoke of it, and have kept our secret because of a promise I made to my sisters and my mother. I have carried this inside me for many years. I sacrificed my life for theirs, but I accept it was my decision. I never wanted anyone to feel sorry for me, I never explained to Rie or my children the total reason why I left, but they know a little more than most people. I thought I was protecting my family, but all I was doing was hurting them. It's funny, as I said before, my brothers and sisters blamed me for what happened in our family, they said I left them, and I was very sad. If I had stayed much longer, I or my father would have died, because we would have tried to kill each other. My father had no rules for himself, but had rules for us, but we could never please him, his rules were for everyone else he used to say, "Don't do as I do, do as I say!" I could never understand why my father did what he did, he said it happened to him. When he was a younger man, he never apologised, as he got older, he would say sorry, but continued as normal. As I grew older, I accepted the way things were. I spoke with my father many times and tried to understand what drove him. When I lived in New York I used to travel home quite a bit, I made a lot of money and always brought presents for everyone. I sent money to help my family because they were my family and I always tried to help and protect them. I never forgot any of them, or their children, and at the drop of a hat, I would be there to help. I loved to see their faces when I would bring something unusual, or get them what they asked for, I never asked for money, I was just happy to help, because I loved my family.

In our lives we have to deal with many problems, but for me, it's not the problem that makes the person, it's the person that solves the problem. It's how you deal with the problem that makes you the person you are, I have dealt with many problems, and in the future I hope I have few or no problems, but realistically I will meet them head on and I will do my best. I have found that every problem has a solution, we just need to find the solution. I hope this book is a solution for somebody's problem when they read it. I hope they realise that they are not alone, and if one person finds the courage to change their situation for the better then I will be happy. Remember abuse comes in many forms, and I have experienced them all, Now I am the power of my life, everyone is in control of their own lives, never give your power away. My mother never took her power, she let my father dominate her, I believe it was possible to change her life many times, but she says she was always afraid, she said my father had threatened to kill us all when we were children, He said he would lock the doors, and pour petrol over us, and burn the house down with us in it. My mother believed him, and she knew he was capable of doing it. Sometimes I think it would have been better for us, the pain and suffering would have been over. To dominate someone is abuse of the highest degree, to have people you are supposed to love and protect live in fear for their lives, is not love.

I called this book 'Surviving Their Love.' This was my mother and father's interpretation of love. Live in fear of death and torture and accept this as the way it is. When I was seven years old, my mother came to me, and asked me to choose who I would stay with, would I stay with my father or go with my mother. I said I would stay with whoever was right, I didn't know what we had was not normal, because we lived in this way. Many years later when I asked my mother why she did not protect us and leave my father, she said it was because I made the decision to stay with my father when I was seven years old, and I was responsible for us staying and for all the abuse we suffered. I could not believe what I was hearing, had she forgotten all the times she stood between me and my father while I tried to protect her, and her holding my hands reminding me of a promise I made when I was twelve years old while he punched and kicked me, also when he was slamming my head into the wall, asking me to keep my promise to her, not to fight back. Every time I tried to protect my mother, he hit me. It wasn't important that she stood between us, he still threw punches and if she got hit, it was her problem, My mother pulled my heart out and stamped it into the floor, now I was responsible for what our father did to us or so she said.

When I was older and played football, sometimes I got hurt, because I was very competitive. One time I had to go to the hospital because I had broken some ribs. The doctor said I had broken a few ribs, I said yes I know I can feel them, the doctor said no not now, before when you were younger, I said I didn't remember, the doctor thought I was joking, because the breaks were very serious. I seriously don't remember. I took many beatings from my father, and my uncle, so it is quite possible it happened in that time. My father spoke with me one time, I asked him why he hurt us so much, he said he didn't remember ever beating us, even then he never took responsibility for his actions. We are all responsible for what we say and do, but we need to learn respect, it is necessary we take care of each other, it's not about who is more powerful, because there is a greater force out there, we think to damage or control someone makes us better or stronger. Believe me something as simple as water can take your life in a second, water can wear out even a rock. We are as fragile as eggs and can be broken easily. we need to understand and control our emotions, and only then it is possible we can be happy. We control emotions every day, but we don't always make friends with them. I had fear for many years, and it drove me crazy, now maybe my fear had foundation, but it ripped my life apart. I would react to situations in many ways, but in fear it was never a rational reaction, You remember when I said I thought the devil used to come to me in the night, and I was afraid of the dark? this was a totally irrational fear as I don't believe in the devil, but as I child the fear was real, when I got married my wife couldn't understand why I left the light on, I was twenty years old, and afraid of the dark, how ridiculous! But I was afraid for more years than that, my fear had foundation, and it was only when I walked the spiritual path, did I realise that there is no devil, there is negative energy, as there is positive energy. What was happening to me, on those dark nights, when I couldn't move, talk, cry, or do anything, when something was in my room lying on top of me, was it an entity or an evil spirit?? The answer is yes, but this entity was both a male and female, playing with me and touching me, having sex with a little innocent child, this was an evil, but a human evil, and it lived in my home with me. So you can see, I did survive their love. I survived sexual abuse, physical abuse, emotional abuse, and most of all, the love of my mother and father. My mother will say this is not true, my father would not have remembered, my aunt is dead, and my uncle is dead also. My younger sister thinks I need counselling, my older sister wants me to be quiet, my brothers didn't know anything, or else they didn't remember. But the biggest insult for me is, they all say I am like my father. In my life, I have never abused or hurt a child in anyway, I protected my children, and spoke about anything they wanted to discuss. I always spoke the truth and when they asked what happened or if their mother did something wrong that made me go away, I always said I was totally responsible for breaking up our family, They are strong, confident, respectful, honest and well developed spiritually, mentally and physically. They don't have the problems their cousins have, with asthma and other congestive conditions. They are independent, there was never any screaming or shouting abuse at them, and they always came before I did.

My sisters hated men, and with good reason, and it's every man, because they were tutored by my mother. every man was wrong, they are all bastards, they are no good, one time My sister spoke to my wives and girlfriends, telling them that I am not a good person to be around, because she was angry with me, she told them that there are two sides to me. I am Dr Jekyll and Mr Hyde in her eyes. This was true to a point I have many sides to me, but never did a woman who was with me ever have to fear for her life, or never did I hurt a child. I have been angry many times, but I walked away, I screamed and shouted, and I have been known to punch walls, I even broke my hand one time. I have never punched a woman or a child. My sisters feared I would tell my partners about the abuse. They were always afraid and rightly so, but I would never hurt my sisters. When my brother's wife left him and moved to Spain, leaving him with his children, it was such a shock to him, it all happened over a week or two. It was a surprise to us all. He asked me to go to Spain with him as he wanted to see his children who were staying awhile with their mother. My parents were now living in Spain, so I agreed to go as I had not seen my parents new house. When I got there, my mother asked me to build a patio at the front of the house, I had only arrived an hour before so I asked if I could have a cup of tea first lol. My brother was gone to see his children. Three days with my mother, I was crazy, my father was quiet, unlike my brother who arrived back and started drinking heavily, he started arguments every night with me, on the third night he asked me to come outside to fight him, I closed the door, he kicked the door in, and started breaking up the apartment. So I went outside with him to try and calm him, in that moment my nephew went for my mother and father, my brother started fighting with me. I moved out of his way, and tried to walk away, he was having none of it, so I picked him up and threw him over a wall, three or four times I put him down and I could have hurt him but he was my brother and I wouldn't hit him. Eventually I put my arms around him to control him, he hit me with his head and broke my cheek bone, and when I wouldn't fight him, he left. My parents arrived back, and the apartment was in bits. I was fixing it up when they came in. My face was swollen and my eye was black, my mother said I was wrong to fight my brother, I told her I had not fought him, I wouldn't have a black eye and a broken cheek bone if I did, she told me I was responsible for all the trouble in our family, I looked past her at my father and said to her that my father was the reason for all the problems not me. My brother was always her favourite, and he could do no wrong. I told her to never speak to me again, I went home the next day.

My father took me to the airport and as we sat and had a coffee together, he said goodbye and for the first time ever he said he was sorry and he loved me, that was the last time we ever spoke, then I went home.

A few days later I went to hospital for an operation on my face. One week had passed and my brother came to the hospital and apologised. About two weeks later, my mother called my home. Eri answered the phone, she said, "It's your mother."

I said, "My mother is dead!" and told Eri to hang up, that was the last time I spoke with my mother or father, for over five years. I never spoke with my father again as he died. I had forgiven so much over the years, and tried to help them, A few years before that happened even before they went to Spain, I ended up standing toe to toe with my father in the street. This time I was bigger and stronger, he said he was going to kill my mother if she did not return some money to him, so I said, "Me First!" and we went outside, again my mother stood between us. My father didn't throw any punches this time, he knew I would kill him. My mother reminded me of my promise to her, I gently moved my mother aside, and stepped up, I was thirty four years old, six foot tall, and weighed nineteen stone, of solid muscle, he was going to die!, My father was fifty five years old, I was going to punch a hole in his chest and hand him his heart! My mother was crying, my sister was pleading with me not to fight, I loved my sister so much and she was so upset I thought she would have a stroke so I kissed her on the forehead and said ok for you I will walk away. I looked at him, and told him he wasn't worth it, I said if I hit you I become you, I walked away, he ran to his car to get an iron bar, as he went towards my car, I laughed and drove away. Now I was the man I wanted to be. I went straight to a car dealership and bought my ex wife and children a new car, I called Rie and asked her to come and pick me up at the garage, she told me my father was at her house looking for me, I told her to tell him to go away from the house as I was in Finglas at the garage, when she came for me my father drove in behind her, I told Rie to take the children into the showroom to look at the cars, I was walking towards my father's car when my mother got out of his car, I asked her what she was doing and she said they were back together, I told her never to call me or speak to me again as I was sick of defending her and she just went back to him, I walked to the car and told my father not to start anything in front of my children and I would meet him anywhere if he still wanted to fight me, he told me that I was right to defend my mother and he respected that. I said I didn't need his approval and he was to take my mother with him and stay away from my family or I would truly kill him. I had broken free from him and his jealous sick mind. I had now been freed from my mother's emotional blackmail, at a great loss and personal cost, I protected this family in all its sick ideas of what family is. For me, I had walked my path, strong, and firm, making mistakes along the way, I was learning to understand what a good man was, because the most important man in a boy's life is his father, and my father was an idiot. The only other men I grew up with were my uncles. One beat the crap out of me, the other one treated me like some sort of a slave, do everything his way, very dominant. when I was sixteen I questioned him on something when we were in the gym, so he challenged me to a strength competition, in front of everyone, of course I took him on and on two of the three exercises I was stronger, he was not happy and he never spoke to me for the next twenty years. He set standards for me, not even he could achieve. My grandfather on my mother's side, was a very violent man, so his sons were also very violent, I didn't know very well, but he left my grandmother when she was a young woman, I only met him three times, the last time I met him he was dying, I made friends with him and stayed with him when he died. He said I was special and he loved me. The uncle who beat me was stealing my grandfather's money, he was charging my grandfather petrol money because he was going to see him, he was taking money from my grandfather's account so he could go out drinking, I took the money and the bank books as my grandfather requested and I was only to give them to my mother, my uncle asked me for the money and I said no, we were in the hospital ward and he got loud and abusive and threatened to beat me if I didn't hand over the money, so I said go for it, I'm not a kid anymore so give it your best shot, he walked away calling me all sorts of names. My grandfather on my father's side, was an absolutely nasty old man or so I was told, he and my father did not get on very well. So the only man I was close to was Pete, my mother's younger brother, he was a father, brother and friend to me, he taught me how to train, he told me the facts of life, he looked out for me, he was my best friend, and I thank him for what he did for me. He had his problems, but he took care of me, our bond was very strong, and I will always be grateful to him. He was a good man, and I was proud of him. May great spirit bless him and keep him safe. This is a man I loved dearly, and I would give my life for him, I would surely have ended up in prison if not for him. He gave me an outlet for my anger, and he helped me build my body, my mind and my confidence. I believe I owed him greatly, he was my friend, my confidant, and one of my mentors.

Please understand I didn't write this book to express my anger, or blame someone for my life, I want you to understand, sometimes life is difficult, but we are only learning, we are here to play, but somewhere we lost our desire to be happy and we got caught up in conditioning. Being happy is an ability we have inside ourselves. Many times, I have heard people say, he or she makes me happy, the idea being someone else makes you happy. I believe when you are happy, you find balance within yourself, you are happy for that time. The possibility that you are happy with someone else's actions is real also. But it's your emotion you feel in that moment, and this applies to all our emotions, we feel what we feel in that specific moment regardless of who we are with, or the place we are in. Sometimes we have perfect balance with the person or place we are in, but it is still our emotion. so many times, I have heard someone say, " I didn't see that coming!" Or one person in the relationship saying, "I was very happy, but I didn't realise my partner wasn't!" we have our own interpretation of every situation, but this is not always equal to someone else's, everybody sees things from their perspective in that moment. So sometimes we have balance with a place, or thing, or reason, and we are happy. When I was a little boy, there were many happy times, I played and laughed with my friends, brothers and sisters, my mother and father. As an adult I've worked with people who have been abused, physically, emotionally, verbally, and sexually, and one thing I understand is, abuse is about power. Some people feel it's necessary to control someone else's life, because they can't control their own. They need to feel they are strong and in control of everything and everyone, but they need to realise people are not toys to be played with as they want. Remember one day a child will become an adult the type of adult will be determined by its teachings. As adults we need to teach our children respect not conditioning. The difference is in conditioning, we teach them our teachings and interpretation of right and wrong, just because it's what we learned does not mean that its correct, it is after all from our perspective. In respect we desire to teach it's necessary we like ourselves and treat people the way we wish to be treated, with honesty and love. Conditioning is the teaching of old experiences and lessons, and respect is a teaching in progress, to respect someone or something, is to feel it inside ourselves, to understand the emotion and to heal it if necessary. Everyone desires happiness, and it's not our place to say when or why. It is as it is. We need to understand this. In nature we need to learn not to change anything, everyone has a different experience in progress. Sometimes we understand and sometimes not. But it's not for us to try and change anyone else, We need to learn from our experiences and let people be themselves, when we meet someone we are attracted to that person for who and what we see, then we get involved, maybe fall in love, they may do something we don't like or behave in a way that we don't like and we start trying to change that person into someone else, when and if they comply we say "you're not the person I met and fell in love with but we are not the same people either. When we meet people, we always put our best foot forward and try to make a good impression. Many times people have asked me, if I was having a good day, for me it's that I'm having a good experience today or maybe not, but when I wake in the morning, and the people I love are good and happy, and when I go to sleep at night and it's the same, also knowing I have done nobody a harm, then it's been a very good day. It's nice to make money, but it's not everything.

This book is about healing, and if it's possible, I am trying to explain why we need to take responsibility for ourselves, we make our decisions inside our minds and sometimes there is an emotional attachment, it is sometimes love, but it can be fear when someone is controlling our experiences in a given situation, or it can be anger when we want to hit back at someone or something. But it is necessary we direct this emotion where it can do most good. We are in control of ourselves. So if someone else wants to take your control away, it is necessary to take it back, look at your fear and realise it's only an emotion, you can control it. Never be afraid to ask for help, if you don't, you will never take control of yourself, or your life. nobody has power over you unless you give it to them.

I want to speak about control, because there are many healers out there who will say, if you have to control yourself you are not free, or if you are controlling an emotion you can't heal it. This is not true, but the only person you should be controlling is you. From my experience I control my anger, for me it's become a friend. My anger works for me, not against me, controlling me. I realise it's only an emotion, and this emotion can be raised or triggered by feelings of insecurities or threats. My answer to this is, try understand what is going on, be responsible for yourself and your actions, so let me give you an example of control, when a beautiful eagle flies towards the ground to catch a rabbit, does he not control his flight? if he doesn't control his descent, he will crash into the ground, killing himself and the rabbit. So control is necessary, if we don't control ourselves we too can crash and burn, destroying everything and everyone around us. So control is not a bad thing, it's only a word to describe an action given to understanding a certain emotion. So why is it necessary to have control, because of the amount of our conditioning and lack of respect we are sometimes taught. you shouldn't just shoot your mouth off with no respect or consideration for what you are saying, word can be devastating and hurtful, so we need to respect other people and their feelings, we don't have to agree or accept what they think or say and it's much easier to just walk away, respond only to the stimulus in front of you, and be mindful, or we will destroy everything around us including what is necessary for our survival. Remember we are emotional beings, sometimes given to moments of madness, but we should try to understand, we need control, just like we need oxygen to survive. Without control we will destroy ourselves.

In this moment I am looking at a beautiful day, the sun is shining, there is a soft breeze and the sound of birds fill the air, there is a beautiful mountain in front of me, green trees and fields, this is where I'm supposed to be in this moment. This is my place, I can't control the day, I am in control of only how I feel. I can only be part of the experience that is this day.

CHAPTER THIRTEEN

My advice to anyone reading this book is, not to focus on the negative experiences, because they were my learning experiences, and remembering that knowledge is a good thing I have learnt well. One day I asked my father why he did what he did, and he told me about his life, it was fairly similar to mine when I was young. For me he was trying to understand why he hurt us so much, When I asked why, and I quote he said, "It happened to me", So from this I can assume for him it was a normal or natural progression. It happened to me so I will teach it to my children. Well, it happened to me, but I did not pass it on to my children, I love them too much to teach them this lesson. Also, they didn't need to experience what I experienced. I always thought when you love someone you do your best for them and try to protect them from all harm, and I believe to harm them yourself by abusing them, is a contradiction to love. When I was older, my father said he loved me, for me it was nice to hear, but it didn't matter anymore. He wrote letters to my brothers and sisters, saying how sorry he was, I never got a letter!!! When he told me he was sorry, I told him, "Tell my brothers and sisters, how sorry you are and try and make up for the pain and hurt you caused them!" My father tried to break the spirit of his children. He succeeded with the rest of the family, but my spirit won't be broken. As a spiritualist and healer, you may well ask if I have forgiven my father and mother for what they did to us. My answer is very simple, it's not for me to forgive them, they need to forgive themselves. For me to say I forgive them, is to say it's okay what you did, and it is not okay to forgive what happened, and I don't forgive them.

Some people will say, "It's what they knew or "It was a learning experience. "They thought they were doing their best, or better still, it's not important, and it's not my place to judge, we all make mistakes. When a person makes a mistake, it's okay, because we all make mistakes. But to repeat your mistake over and over, I don't think it's a mistake it's a habit. I don't judge my parents or family for what they do or did, or how they live their lives, but I live my life my way, and yes I have made my mistakes, but I have learned from them, and tried never to repeat them. My parents continued to live as they have always lived, they lived with the fear of their secrets. My father was still a victim, with a victim mentality and a feeling of being owed something but they were happy with their behaviour!!! I can never forgive, because I don't understand why, I bare no grudges, if they were happy, that's good, they have to deal with their conscience, and they would have had to be able to sleep at night. I would do no harm to my family, and I am always here to help them when they need me, but I will ask for nothing from them, I don't need to forgive anything or anyone, only myself. I can understand it's simple to make mistakes, as I said before, this is a learning experience and we learn from our mistakes. I understand the desire to kill someone, to fight back, or steal, to make problems for someone who may have hurt me in some way, but to hurt innocent children from as early as three years old and younger, is beyond my understanding and forgiveness.

CHAPTER FOURTEEN

I spoke earlier about great spirit, for me I walk my path with great spirit (God) I have practised the Native American way and spiritual path for many years, and one thing I have learnt is that I am responsible for what I say and do. It's my decisions and my thoughts and actions. So, I try to do my best every day, I thank great spirit for my experiences every day, and I ask him/her to bless my children and the people I love. I practice ceremony, and it has taught me responsibility for myself, and respect for everyone and everything. This planet was here before you and I, the rocks, plants and animals, then us, when we came, we began to destroy everything. We do not understand or care and this has continued and is continuing, so who is it controlling this journey? If we continue in this way, we will destroy ourselves. Man is a very dangerous animal. It's quite possible we will blow ourselves up. The planet is alive, and it is breathing, it has a heart just like you and me. We don't own this planet, we are only a part of it, But because we do not value life, we are not interested, we can use its resources until there is nothing left, I have an Indian poster on my wall that reads: Only after the last animal has been killed, only after the last tree has been cut, only after the last fish has been caught, only then will we realise that money cannot be eaten. Never have I read anything so true, we have seen what the planet has given us, and we still persist in killing it. I think we are living in the time of the Antichrist, but it's not any person or thing, it is the human race, but many people don't care and seem to think nothing is going to happen. All we need to do is sit back, wait, and continue in the same fashion. Nostradamus said, "The Antichrist would appear as a peace maker, after balls of fire hits the new city." Well I can think of two people who are in a position to destroy mankind, and in this time they both speak of peace, they are both arrogant idiots, with little minds, but they have the power and ability to destroy us all. They have the nuclear weapons at the ready, and are playing with the lives of billions of people, if one of them makes the first strike, they will die also, and killing billions of people, animals and nature itself, but nature will survive, it has survived the dinosaurs extinction, it will survive ours.

This is a time of great fear all over the world. We are destroying our world in the name of progress. When are we going to realise that this planet is fighting back? And if you look at our weather, you can see this. We are having floods of mega proportions, earthquakes, volcanoes, and much, much more. The seas are claiming back the land, the waters are rising, and I think there is a need to do something about this. All over the world, we are claiming nature, we are killing all our rainforests, it is the trees that provide our oxygen, the plant that feed us and the animals that serve us so well. We have killed so many things that are necessary for our survival, and we are being controlled by people and things that don't have a clue. The Native Americans foretold all this, they foretold that it would be a benefit to all the people and nations of this planet to remember what is natural, to respect all nature and ask the spirit in all things to forgive our selfishness and stupidity. We need to survive the love for ourselves. Because we love ourselves so much, we are killing ourselves, and all because we can and for no other reason, every animal on this planet has a primal instinct to survive, they kill only what is necessary for their survival. and the survival of their families. The also do a great favour by maintaining equilibrium on this planet. It is the human animal that destroys everything in its path. We are like a virus, we spread and multiply and destroy everything we touch, and with no consideration for coming generations. If we don't understand it, we kill it. If it's necessary for that moment destroy it, if it's in our way, eliminate the problem be it human, animal or plant, or planet, we are killing everything, forgetting it cannot be replaced or reproduced. At the rate we are killing is making everything extinct, and if we don't stop, we will also be extinct. So what is the answer?

It is my belief, that everything is important to our survival, and I know there are many more people trying to do and respect the spirit life force in everything. We need to learn from past experiences, and if we blow up the planet, I am certain it will survive, but we won't, God only knows where we will be. Years ago, they made movies about sending people into space, now we actually do it, in those days it was called science fiction, now it's reality. Now they make movies about nuclear destruction, about the end of humankind. I ask you, do you really think this is science fiction? I don't! To survive the love for ourselves, we need to return the love to our planet, we are connected to our planet and everything on it. We need to learn a new way to love. To love this planet, is to love ourselves. To protect ourselves is to protect everything on this planet, so now we are back to our conditioning. we are taught to be selfish, insecure, happy, sad, loving, hateful, controlling idiotic, we only really need to cultivate three of those things - Respect, love and self control. It is not necessary to control the love, we only need to control our insecurities around love, and to do that we need to understand what love really is.

The word love is used in everything, so I think it has lost its meaning It is used to describe a feeling, emotion want or desire, "I would love an ice cream!" or, "I would love to do this or that!" The word love is used everywhere. So can we feel love? I think we can, or it is only affection for someone or something. When we speak of how we love someone, we describe an emotion of great strength, but are there so many different kinds of love, you love your parents, brothers, sisters, friend, animal, lover, and many other things, so what determines the depth of love for someone or something. I think it's a matter of importance, and relationship the more important someone is to you or your life, the more you feel for them, and the stronger your love is. The people most important to us generally are our family, so we learn how to love from them. But love is natural, it is part of what and who we are. We don't need to learn to love, we need only to learn how to express love. The love for a man and a woman is equal, but we express it very differently, this is where our family have the most influence, and this is where we learn the conditioning for love. This is our conditioning - learning. So now let's look at conditional love. When you are little and you do something good, you receive affection (love) and when you are not good, you receive a clip around the ear, this is not love. The most important person in my life when I was young, was my grandmother, she taught me unconditional love, when I made mistakes, or did something wrong, she loved me equal and always expressed it.

As I grew, I learnt the conditions for love. If you were good to me, I loved you, and I learnt to manipulate people. My mother said if I loved her, I would be a good boy, and my father said if I was not a good boy, he would kill me. So, I learnt to be a good boy, sometimes the hard way. My mother spoke so much how she disliked my father, and my father beat my mother, but they stayed together because they said they loved each other, So even in that way, I learnt to accept that love has its ups and downs and it had a price, so now it's okay to stay with someone you don't even like because you love them? and it's okay to control the life of someone and treat them like dirt, because you love them? You can be totally unhappy, but it's the price of love. So now I understood price of love. For me when I began to date women, I thought it was okay to be a total idiot. I accepted all sorts of crap, and I gave an equal amount back, but this was love and this behaviour was acceptable for love or some feeling of love. It took years for me to understand that love is endless, and it has no boundaries or conditions. love just is.

My grandmother died when I was eighteen years old, I still feel the love we shared. My first wife and I still love each other, and we have had many problems. But the love for my children is total and unconditional.

Sometimes they make mistakes, and my love never changes, we have had arguments, and our love never changed. So it is possible to have unconditional love. To love unconditionally, takes great strength, belief and trust, firstly in yourself, and then in the person you love. To believe in yourself is most important, you need to value yourself and realise that what you say, and what you feel is very important. You need to Believe you deserve to be happy, trust your judgement in people, and go with your instincts, your feelings and emotions are yours and it's your decision to express them. It takes a lot of practice, but it's a lesson worth learning. One time I went sky diving, and the feeling was the best in the world. I had fear, excitement, and I experienced many other emotions as the ground raced towards me, it was amazing! then I opened my parachute and the feeling of total peace was beautiful. I had time to enjoy the experience as I floated to the ground, and then it was back to the ground and reality. It was one of the most beautiful experiences I have ever had, but the best experiences I have ever had was when I saw my children enter this world. my children were my gifts.

About a year after my second wife went back to Chile, I met an Italian lady, I went to the Arthur Finlay College in Stanstead in the UK. I was always pulled back to my spiritual path. Doni was one of the most beautiful women I had ever seen, and I fell in love with her. So for a few years I was peaceful and spiritual, I had received my spirit name in a sweat lodge many years before, and it is a name I was proud to wear, I was called Grey Wolf Spiritual Warrior, and I was a warrior for sure. Everybody called me 'Wolf.' A warrior is not violent man, he is a protector of his family and clan, he will stand for what is right. He can fight but will only do so when there is no other option. I slipped in and out of my spiritual ways, but I longed for peace inside my life, I had looked for love all my life, I wanted someone who could love a broken man, but my fear always won. When I had something good, I would not trust. I would ruin it; I would look for reasons to get out. If you touched my heart, I ran as far away as fast as I could, and I was never faithful to anyone for a very long time. As soon as I felt something, or if I felt scared I would mess things up, I was with Doni for 12 years, and for the first few years everything was beautiful, we had our problems but what we shared was amazing, we loved each other and I tried to live in Italy, and she tried to live in Ireland. We had an argument and she went home, she met some guy and moved into his home, she didn't even know this man. I was so angry, then he began to cause problems for her, so she called me and I went to Italy and I went to sort him out. Doni and I got back together but I lost trust in her, I had affairs and fucked around, so it was not long until I lost Doni, we are still friends nineteen years later and we accept and love each other, when I met Doni in Stanstead hall it was an amazing experience. When we split up, I went back to the violent life again. I liked the turmoil, the aggression, the fear. But most of all I liked to hit bullies. I would never back down, but I would give the other guy an opportunity to walk away, but the bullies always had to fight. I would not let them walk away

CHAPTER FIFTEEN

This is how I met Doni. My friend asked me to go to London with him for a weekend of drumming and Indian ceremony, I had no money having just come back from Chile. So I told my friend I couldn't go. but he very kindly paid for my plane ticket, and my ex wife Rie gave me money to take part in the workshop. Five days before we were due to go, I was not going to go. After a lot of nagging and persuasion I decided to go. As we arrived in Stanstead Hall, we were in the waiting area waiting to sign in, I saw four women, one of which was Doni, I did not get good look at her, but I felt her. We went into the room with them to sign in, and when she spoke, I just looked at her, she was speaking Italian. I didn't understand a word she said. When we registered, we all went to eat. My friend and I sat at the same table as the Italians, and one of them could speak English. We all introduced ourselves, and then another person came to our table. It was David, a very gentle special man. He made a big impact in my life, but I will speak of him later. David sat beside me on the right, and Mark was on my left. Beside him was Donatella (Doni). There was one chair facing Doni, not being used, so I was determined to sit there at the next meal. I couldn't take my eyes of her, I had this urge to walk up to her and kiss her, ask her where she had been for so long. I felt I knew her, and I loved her so much, but in reality, I had just met her, and if I did not control myself, I would make a total idiot of myself. So the next meal, I sat facing her, and as the meal progressed, I asked her to marry me. First there was silence, and then everyone laughed, and she said no I was crazy, but then there was silence again, and I asked her again. She looked at me and smiled a smile that nearly knocked me to the floor. The she said if I come to Italy, she would say yes. I said okay, I would come to Italy soon. We ate and continued with Angela translating for everyone. Angela was her friend. I couldn't take my eyes off her, she had beautiful strong features, her hair long and black with beautiful green brown eyes, she looked like an Apache Indian, I never felt so much love for another person in this way. To my surprise, I never even thought about sex. I just wanted to look at her, and if possible, hold her hand. We went for a walk that night, she walked with Mark and I talked to Angela, Mark gave it his best shot, but she never gave him an inch. I asked her to walk with me alone, she said no and went inside. I was so disappointed, I couldn't sleep, I thought about her all night.

The next day, she stayed beside me all day, she held my hand, and stayed close. We worked on ceremony together, she smiled and agreed when I asked her to drum for me, Mark was really pissed off, for me it was a natural choice. He said he was my friend and I had only met Doni the day before, I felt I knew her for all my life, and we were always together. Doni didn't speak a word of English, I had no Italian, but we communicated, the next day, we were going home, I was going for my plane. Doni came to reception and asked me to go with her, I felt like I knew Doni from another lifetime, and on Sunday morning we did ceremony and then we had to say goodbye, I did what she asked, and I went to her room. She kneeled on the floor in front of me as I sat on the bed, she tried to thank me for the time we spent together that weekend. She wrote a note and asked me to translate it when I got home. I got up to leave, and as I looked back at her she looked sad. I put my arms around and held her, I felt I was leaving part of me behind. I was so nervous as was she, so eventually I worked up the courage to kiss her, when I kissed her she took my breath away, as I kissed her I felt light headed and all over the place, I was dizzy and my heart was pumping so hard and fast, it was amazing, then I realised I was not breathing, so when the kiss was finished I took a huge breath in and we laughed, I forgot to breathe, the experience was like my parachute jump. It's the best way to describe it. I was afraid and then the rush, then the quiet, and then the reality. I had to leave to go home. I would sooner have left my right arm. When I got home, I tried to phone Doni at Stanstead airport, it took nearly two hours, but I got to speak to her. I went to Italy two weeks later, and we were together twelve years, we had some good times, and some not so good times, but our problems were little compared to our love. Most of our problems were in difficulty with communication, but the love is still the same, and it's been nineteen years now and our love is perfectly strong and secure when I look at this woman I just melt inside, she has a beautiful heart, she has experienced the same experiences from the female perspective. Her life has run an equal course to mine, the problems I experienced in my life, she experienced in her life. Also, she did not want to go to Stanstead where we met and it was her friends who persuaded her to go and they paid for her ticket also, what a coincidence!!! This woman is my angel, with a love and a heart so true, I trust Doni completely, because she completes me, she is still my best friend When I was in Stanstead, I met David, this man is my friend, and I am so honoured, he is my friend, he has a heart true and gentle he has the qualities one day I hope to have. He is funny, sincere, and full of love and compassion. He has the heart of a beautiful child, inspired by everything, and willing to learn and love. My wish for this man is for a gentle life, full of love may his every dream come true, in beautiful colour, and I love you with good intention. I am your friend; I am here when you need me. So now I hope you can understand, that love is unconditional, it is peaceful and secure. It can't be measured, or weighted and contains no fear. So love with all your heart, ask for nothing, but give your all, when you fall in love you will know. You can't touch it or see it, you can only feel it, it is a beautiful feeling full of beautiful emotions, love just is. To love in this way, is true love.

I was in my forties by now, I was fit and strong and up for it. Inside me was a child longing for acceptance and a man looking for peace. As a healer I am very present when I work at my healing work. I found peace; I had many amazing experiences my life was happy. I was working my stuff out, I have worked with lots of people and helped many, as much as they have helped me. I was given a beautiful gift, I am an intuitive natural healer, I learnt the Native American way, I did the work, I did the ceremonies, I hurt, I released, I prayed, I worked with a lot of healers over the years. Some were good, some were very good, but some do a course and believe they are Gods, or Goddesses. Goddesses is a term used by many Reiki healers, I spent time with these people and some of them are having a laugh. On many occasions, I was told that if we slept together, we would be a stronger force, what a load of bull! They talk about forgiveness, but many are full of ego and hold onto grudges, more so than most of the healers I have worked with. In General, I work alone, and my opinion is, we are all healers, it's just some practice more than others. Nobody is better than anyone else, a healing is as simple as a smile making someone smile can change their whole day. The forgiveness end of things is another story, we don't need to forgive anyone who has wronged us, we need to forgive ourselves for whatever we perceive ourselves to be, weak, stupid, or not good enough, so just let the stuff go, and move on. We never really get over the betrayal or the hurt, but we should try to come to terms with it, forgive ourselves and let it go, holding it and dealing with it just upsets us and our lives.

As usual, I go back to the violence, back on the doors dealing with all the stress that came with it. Then a series of events over the next few years changed how I saw things; I have been in many fights and confrontations. I have been hit many times. So black eyes, bruises, pulled muscles etc are things I got used too, the pain and the violence were familiar, but things were starting to change, and I believe spirit was telling me it's time to stop. I had two hits put on me by drug dealers, and still I went back. Now spirit was going to take this to another level. I was standing at a door in Wicklow, Blessington to be exact. There were two of us on the door, me and Will. A fight broke out inside the club and the couple were brought out, as was the usual format for me, I always dealt with it at the door. Anyway, we got them out and I sent the other security personal inside. I was dealing with it as usual, I became aware, that there was a bit of a gathering outside on the road, now there was eight guys and one girl. I said to Will we were in for it, so I called for support, and then it kicked off. Before help arrived, I was fighting four guys, one guy rugby tackled me and picked me up and slammed me into the wall, the other three were throwing punches, and Will had the other four on him, when the support finally arrive, there was eight on eight, the fight broke up, and I was standing there with a terrible pain in my forehead, my friend Kev said, "Wolf, your nose is broken!" I laughed and said yeah ok, but it was, so I had to put it back in place, I cannot describe the pain I felt. I had never had my nose broken before, only a few bones in my hand from fighting, so now I had a broken nose and two black eyes, The price of my job. Over the next seven years, my injuries got worse. I got four broken ribs, a dislocated shoulder, jaw broken, eye socket smashed, and a very bad knee injury that put me out of action for over a year. But I am a stubborn Gobshite, and I didn't see the pattern, but the injuries were more severe each time, and my ability to do my job was compromised. I was told that the facial injury trauma was so severe, I should have died, and another hit like that would kill me. Spirit was sending me a message. My family asked me to stop, but not me, no, I would never be able to live with myself if I was afraid. So I went back time and time again, and eventually I got the message.

I met another woman, and what a woman! She was Romanian, and very beautiful, I fell totally in love with her, her name was Lauren, and I really loved her. I was with her for three years. When I would come home at night, she would be awake waiting for me, she'd say, "Are you okay babe?"

And I'd say, "Yes beautiful I am okay, no injuries tonight." Then I would sit on the bed and just smell her, I'd kiss her, I couldn't wait to get home to her, I was so in love with her, she just couldn't see it, We were together for three years and I never as much looked at another woman. I knew she was the only one I wanted to be with. One night this beautiful black girl asked me to take her home, I told her I had a girlfriend and she said Lauren was a lucky woman, but I loved Lauren. She would go out with her friends and even one of her ex boyfriends used to pick her up, I was a little jealous, but I never let it interfere with us, I trusted her, I was in love, I was happy. We had our own problems as lots of people do but I was willing to try and sort things out, I had realised that my past had cost me so much. Not so much because of what happened, but because of how I allowed it to affect me. I was making headway at least. I was beginning to trust, I was allowing love into my life, I had a long way to go. But I had Lauren, my children were grown, and I had grandchildren. I had great relationships with all who were close to me. There was tension with my brothers and sisters, because I didn't speak to my mother, but that didn't phase me much I was working and there was plenty of money. Lauren and I were doing okay, we had holidays and were having a good time or at least I thought so, we had our ups and downs, She was very insecure, but I thought she would settle when she saw how much I loved her. She had little tantrums, here and there, but it was okay. My daughter was getting married, so it was all good. My son was training in the gym with me, happy chappy! Then I got the very bad knee injury, and this really messed things up. When I shattered my knee, I was taking a guy out of the restaurant beside the club where I worked. I misjudged three steps, myself, this guy, and two Russian bouncers, came down on my knee, I spent the next year getting back on my feet. Things became tough, as money was tight. I became very frustrated and angry, Lauren and I started to fight more. My daughter's wedding was getting close, and I was very stressed, I felt like I was letting another part of me go. I was losing my baby girl, Lauren was giving me shit, her son was causing problems, her ex husband was an asshole also making problems, my uncle was on my case, he and Lauren were not talking, they had a fallout he said I should walk away from her, he and I had a fallout, my daughter didn't invite my family to the wedding so that caused some issues, I was hurt and money was tight, so I had a lot going on, and true to form I closed everyone off, I was struggling in life, I thought, "Jesus can it get any worse!" Then my friend John called me and offered me some work, he owns a patio centre. The work was tough, I was working for John a couple of days a week. My knee was in a bad way, so John gave me easy work. It began to get a bit stronger, and I began to feel a bit better now I was making some money again. John also gave Lauren some work, so that took some of the stress away. I was waiting for a knee operation; I was in pain every day. the day finally came for my operation, and Lauren and I were fighting again. She wanted to come to the hospital with me and I said no, because she needed to be home for her son who would be coming home from school. She was really pissed off. When I came home after my operation, the atmosphere was picture and no sound! I was too sore to argue, so I went to bed for three days, she was really mad at me and didn't even talk to me for those three days. she wouldn't cook for me so I had to get up and sort myself out, or I would have been starving also, what a nightmare. On the fourth day, as soon as I could put my boots and jeans on, I left. On the fifth day I went back for our engagement ring. If she wasn't marrying me, she wasn't keeping the engagement ring. we had only got engaged at Christmas. I was so angry with her. I threatened to throw her TV over the balcony, because she told me she had sold the ring, I was furious. I forgot how intimidating I could be, but she stood toe to toe with me on several occasions and was never afraid before, she then went to my friends and lied about what happened, saying she was afraid of me, and if she was scared, then for that I truly apologise, I still love her very deeply, since we broke up and to this day, she still won't talk to me. I have apologised. she says that she is not angry with me but every time I try to make peace, she is rude and snappy, Lauren knew that I would never put a hand on her but she loved the drama of it all, it was a very stressful time for us both, and I really do wish her all the best,

My daughter called me, and said she wanted to talk to me, she told me I would not be walking her down the aisle, I was devastated, not only did I feel I was losing a part of me, but now I couldn't even give her away at her wedding. She also told me that none of my family were allowed to attend the wedding. I thought, "What is happening in my life!" Everything was great the year before. I told my daughter, that if that is what she wanted then I would go along with it. One day my son and I were coming back from the Gym, he said to me, "Mam and his sister, are worried about me being at the wedding." I didn't get on with my ex wife's family, but I said I didn't care about what they might do or say, as my baby girl was getting married. My son told me that his mam wanted to do up the house, and back garden for the wedding, and he asked if I could help him. So I did the work and he helped me. I finished it two days before the wedding. The night before the wedding, we were sitting laughing and joking. The day of the wedding, my family turned their backs on me. My daughter had said it was a small private wedding, that's why none of my brothers and sisters where invited. But every one of my ex wife's aunts and uncles, and all her family were there at the wedding, including nephews and nieces, also her friends. I was floored. My daughter never spoke two words to me, my ex ignored me, my son was in the middle. My ex father in law, put it up to me twice, but I stayed calm. My ex sister in law kicked off wanting to know why I was at the wedding. I was broken, my heart once again betrayed by my family. I left at twelve o'clock and have not spoken to them since. I am not allowed to see my grandchildren, and my son's wife won't let me see her children. To this day, I have had no explanation. I taught my son that men stand alone, and sheep run in herds, never stand by and let an injustice be done. They know I did nothing wrong to them, all I ever did was give them my best, so once again I was floored.

My family betrayed me again for the second time in my life I was torn apart. Even in my darkest hour when I wanted to commit suicide, I held on for them. I didn't want to leave them with the aftermath of something like that. So if I died in a fight, that was another thing. And after all these years, I was on my knees, and broken for the second time. My world fell apart, I'd lost Lauren, and now my I had lost my family. The only reason I'm here, heartbroken and in pain. I wanted to hit out and cause so many problems, we had arguments, and disagreements throughout our lives, but this was unforgiveable. I was so angry and hurt. I felt betrayed. So why did this happen again? Was I so unlovable? My parents couldn't have loved me, not doing what they did, and yet I am supposed to forgive them? My children, who taught them to be so stubborn and hard? Did I not break the circle? what was going on in my life? I could understand Lauren, because she is not my blood, but my children they are mine. They are my blood. I always told them, that family comes first, so what is going on? I know what it is. It's their mothers fault, her family is to blame, my children spent lots of time with my in-laws who I hated with a passion I should have stopped my kids seeing their grandparents, their grandmother had no forgiveness in her, she was a bitter old woman right to the end, she always belittled me to my children, what a witch! but hang on! she was angry with me because of her little girl, I hurt Rie, and I would be the same if someone hurt one of mine, I would be angry too. I taught my children to stand up and speak their minds, right or wrong. They were doing what I taught them, their anger was theirs, and they felt they had reason. So who was I to say they are wrong. Life is seen from our own perspective. It's how we see things, so their anger was fuelled by their perception, they are angry with me because I had left them when they were young. My son told me he had it so hard growing up, because I wasn't there, that is his perspective on things, for me I was always there, and just a phone call away. I would have been there in a moment. My daughter is a drama queen, so her perspective on things is also different. My ex-wife knows the truth, and she knows they always came first, it was always her and the children first, even at the expense of my own life and happiness. I didn't deserve to be happy. I had hurt my wife, and my children, I left them, my reasons didn't matter. As far as I was concerned, I was not worth anything, and I deserved everything I got. A few years before I met Lauren, I asked my ex-wife to get back together, after all that had happened, we were still good and loved each other very much, even through all the heartache we had been sleeping together since the day we got married. All the years, and all the affairs, she was the only constant in my life. We were dating and sleeping together, and she seemed happy. So one day I asked her can we try again, she said no, and that was the last time we slept together. I wasn't happy but I had to accept it. Years later my son said I was angry with his mother because she turned me down, he had noticed a change between his mam and me, because we didn't go out anymore, and the relationship had changed. His mother told him I was pissed off she said no to me. The truth is yes, I was hurt, I thought we were somewhere else in our relationship, so I told him the truth. His mam said I was lying, he believed her. To this day she denies she was having a sexual relationship with me, so prim and proper, but what a lying hypocrite she has become.

One day I was alone, feeling like shit, I was standing in my kitchen looking out to the garden, hurt and angry. I wanted to just disappear or run away. I was watching the trees sway, and a peace came over me, I realised that it's okay if they are angry with me, or if they deny me, I still love them. This love is what I am, it is who I am. All my life I looked for it, in the approval of others, In relationships, in places and things. But I am love, it's not outside me. It's okay for them to feel and be what they want. How they believe me to be or their perception of me, and the situation is their perception of life. So that's how they see it. I know I did nothing wrong; I only did my best for them. I kept them safe, well clothed and fed, and every day I told them I loved them in every way I could, I am proud of them, if they are angry or annoyed with me, that's okay, because I love them, the love is mine. I am love, it's not outside me and nobody can give it to me.

CHAPTER SIXTEEN

One thing I have learnt, is that love never changes, People do, love is the one constant in our lives, we search for it, we long for it, and we miss it when we perceive it to be gone or missing. But love never goes away, relationships change, and people go away, so just love yourself. And one day you will share it again, but love is me, and I am loveable. My spiritual path has taught me what is important, and nothing is personal, other people have feelings, and their feelings are theirs, so it's not personal. How they feel about me, is not my feelings, so therefore it's not personal. My father taught me many things, but most of all he taught me to be kind, despite how he treated me. My father was a victim because he was not secure enough to break the cycle of abuse. It was done to him and he passed it forward onto me. I didn't want my children to know or experience what I had, so it stopped with me. As a boy, I was always afraid, I never knew what was going to happen next, but I would defy my father whenever I could. Sometimes he would find out, sometimes he wouldn't. When he died, we hadn't spoken for five years, my family were devastated. I didn't understand this, I stood by his coffin, my brother was crying, and asked me what we were going to do now, I said it's okay, I am here, and we will just keep going. I saw the love for this man in my brothers and sisters, but I just couldn't understand it at that time. My father was so lucky, even after all he had done, he was loved, this was a testament to my brothers and sister's strength of character, they have the ability to love, and love without condition.

I spoke to my father as he lay in the coffin, I wished him well on the next part of his journey, I said goodbye to him and I tried to forgive him for his indiscretions, and all the hurt that he had caused me and my family. I thought I made my peace. But to my surprise and after feeling all spiritual and calm, I was very angry he got away with all he had done, his secrets died with him. We were left with the aftermath, the anger inside me festered. So back to my cycle of violence again, back on the doors, fighting again, still spiritual, still meditating, calm on the outside, but raging on the inside. I did my job, and I did it well. Injury after injury, I kept going. When my father's name was spoken, I would get so angry. People who knew him would say, how great he was. Because I was keeping secrets, I would try to smile on the outside, but the inside I wanted to say, what a complete asshole he was. So this forgiveness thing was not working for me. But then the penny dropped, I didn't need to forgive him, I needed to forgive myself, there is no healing in secrets. Those of us who have been abused, we need to remember, we were not responsible for the things that were done to us, the pain, the humiliation, inflicted on innocence, by people with no empathy, for reasons that we cannot comprehend, sadly done by people we trusted and loved, in many cases. Abuse is abuse, in all its guises, we were lied to and manipulated to satisfy some need or desire to have power and victimise us. Many of us lost our childhoods, spent so much time in fear, living with terror of what was coming for us. Those people who should have loved us, this little boy or girl, crying out for love, and approval, the child inside every one of us. It's time to take back the control and reclaim our innocence. Make the child feel loved and safe, it's your choice now, you are in control, So love yourself, this is your life so change it, live it, and be happy. The scars of abuse never go away, so learn to cope with them in such a way that you are no longer destructive to your own life. Stop getting in your own way because of your past, it can't be changed, but we can teach ourselves a new way. So live happy, let yesterday go, forget tomorrow and live today as happily as you possibly can. This is your life, so live it.

The abuse I endured has affected many aspects of my life, all my relationships in my life have been tainted, my emotional being is like a rollercoaster, I have loved, lusted, and lost. I am no saint, I had many affairs, I cheated, on all my partners, except Lauren, I loved her so much, but then I loved them all. When she asked why I was faithful to her, I used to say, I have grown up, it has taken years and years, to get here. My belief system is very different, my trust issues vary from person to person, and that depends on my relationship with that person. Am I healed? to be honest, I am still healing, the scars are still there, memories of the wounds inflicted over many years. They will never truly heal but as long as I don't focus on them, I am in control. Helping others helps me heal. But I am a better man. The years have taken their toll, but I am still strong, just lots of aches and pains, I am stronger emotionally, I make better choices and my life is great. Just because my father was an idiot, doesn't mean I have to be one.

So every day I try to make good choices, I am a little less hard on myself. The people who abused me, don't get my forgiveness, I get that! So I try to be good to myself, I try not to let the stuff control my life, not make decisions, based on emotions. I am fair with myself, but when I make mistakes, I don't come down hard on myself. I so want to help others, and I just need your permission. I am Grey Wolf Spirit Warrior. I have lived a life with many experiences, some great, and some not so great. I have travelled the world and seen many beautiful places. I have endured abuse, loss and pain. Sometimes I just wanted to leave this place, I have felt disappointed, and cheated, I lived inside my head, sometimes in total despair, I was battered, beaten, abused, and victimised. Through all of this, even when the devil came to me at night and abused my little body, my terror at this heavy being, hot breath on my neck, my face pushed into the pillows, being so frightened and helpless, I couldn't even call out.

For years I had night terrors, reliving it over and over again, I fought back. I tried to look over my shoulder to see who it was. Little by little I turned my head, so frightened, so scared, even into adulthood. I fought it, I cursed it, I cried it and I prayed, and I faced my fear. My body was broken, smashed to pieces, my mind terrified, I was going to see what it was. Even as a big strong man, I was taken back to the fear.

My grandmother told me I was her special boy, she believed in me, she loved me, someone loved me, I had to see what it was. I grew big and strong, so I could beat the shit out of my father, but this thing that came in the night, brought me back to the little boy who was so scared of the dark, even into my adult years, my married years, I could not sleep with the lights off, the psychological effects of not being able to fight this thing was devastating, I was afraid of what came in the dark. I couldn't protect my children, my wife, because it rendered me helpless and frozen in fear, I was a man, I had to protect them, they saw me as invincible, I couldn't let them down. I was big and strong, afraid of no man, but this thing, this fear, was controlling all aspects of my life. I prayed for it to stand in front of me, I was turning my head little by little, "Fuck you!!! I am going to face you!!!! I will see your face!!" So many years of torment, and then I turned, I saw the devil, and my heart shattered. I accepted the physical, emotional and mental abuse, I dealt with the torture, and punishments, but everything changed the night I saw the face of the devil. The Native Americans way has taught me to have courage and face fear. To stand for family and loved ones, to be the best version of myself. To love completely, with no condition, to have integrity, respect, and honour.

So today, I stand as my own man. I have problems just like everyone else, I have trust issues, I have fears, some days are good, some days are not so good. But every day I put my feet on the floor, my loved ones are strong and healthy, I am having a great day. I will do my best; this is my life and I own it. Surviving their love wasn't easy, but I am still here. I am not dead yet! To Rie and my children, I love you, my grandchildren I adore you, I am always here.

Love is all that matters, but you must love in such a way, that you love completely, with no conditions, but the love begins and ends with you. Forgive yourself first, for whatever reason you feel you were not good enough. I can never forgive my father for his actions, because I don't understand why he did the things he did. He said it was because it was done to him, but it was done to me too, and I didn't do it to mine. I forgave myself, for not being big and strong enough to stop him from hurting us. When I was big enough, I could have beat him to a pulp but then I would have been just like him, and I am not him. I have come a long way, from there and I would like to think that my life was a lesson. I want to help others to understand that there is a way forward, just believe in yourself. The only person you need to forgive is yourself. Change the way you think, every thought in your mind is yours, so think highly of yourself. Remember you are in the driving seat, now you are in control, and it's your decisions that you make. So make good ones that serve your life. It is your life after all, if you can't forgive, then you must let go, and move forward, in a positive way, the past is over, learn and let go. My father is dead, my mother is alive, living her misery, my siblings are all good, doing their best, we all survived their love.

PROLOGUE

Where am I today? you may ask. I am in a very good place. The anger for myself is gone, I don't blame myself anymore. Sometimes I remember things, but I don't focus on the bad stuff, but I am my own man now. I make my decisions, this is my life, I am happy with parts of my life, and sometimes I am sad. The abuse I endured has left scars and scars are a constant reminder, sometimes I might have an experience that rubs on my scars and it can trigger a negative reaction, I have to be mindful in these moments or I can allow myself to be drawn into the drama. every day I get out of bed and I'm grateful for another day of life, today I will do my best, memories are always there, but that's the past, so I try to live in this moment, I don't think we ever heal completely, but we can try not to be negative or allow it to hurt us, healing is about finding peace with yourself it's not about erasing the past, it's coming to terms with it, in such a way that you are no longer self-destructive. Writing this book has brought up so many things, it has been helpful in aiding my healing, I have relived some of the memories. Sometimes I mourn the loss of innocence and wish things had been different, but I believe my life went as it was supposed to. My life experiences have brought me to this moment. I am free, and I am me, I like the man I am, and I am a work in progress, I hope I can help those enduring abuse to teach them to take back their power, and be the best version of themselves. I wish to guide people to their own healing. Scars leave a mark, a memory, we don't have to live in that memory, we can acknowledge the memory and let it go, especially if it no longer serves us. If you are lucky enough to wake up and get out of bed then you're having a good day, the rest is up to you, so give it your best, it's your life so edit and rewrite your own story and make it a love story.

I am a I Shamanic Healer/Councillor, Reiki Healer, Psychic Councillor, empath, medium and gravity practitioner. Abuse is devastating, in all forms, I hope this book will be of some help to those, who need it. We never quite get over being abused, it's a bit like losing someone we love, we mourn them, we mourn ourselves and any loss we feel, but we just learn to cope we learn to live with it and as long as we don't let the loss control us and understand it's our life and our decision.

This is my life; I am in charge.

I am Grey Wolf. The Spirit Warrior.

Your life story is written by you so write it well.

You are in control, so take responsibility for yourself.

Every problem has a solution, so find your solutions.

There is no healing in secrets, speak and ask for help.